God's Greatest Holy Nation

Abraham???

United States of America

Note to reader

The famed Abrahamic covenant comes from Genesis 12:1-3 and 28:14-15. It reads:

"Now the Lord said to Abram, 'Go from your country and your kindred and your father's house to the land that I will show you. And I will make you a great nation, and I will bless you and I will make your name great, so that you will be a blessing. I will bless those who bless you, and curse those who curse you. All the families of the earth shall find blessing in you." To Jacob: I, Yahweh, am the God of Abraham your father, and the God of Isaac. The ground on which you are lying I shall give to you and your descendants. Your descendants will be as plentiful as the dust on the ground; you will spread out to west and east, to north and south, and all clans on earth will bless themselves by you and your descendants. Be sure, I am with you; I shall keep you safe wherever you go, and bring you back to this country, for I shall never desert you until I have done what I have promised you.'

Abraham was a real person who lived somewhere around 2100 BC. It has been 4124 years since God proclaim the Covenant to Abraham. It is time this Covenant come to pass. In America there are 235,151,203 Christians who believe in Christ whilst in Israel 7,208.000 Jews who deny Christ. You think God's Greatest Nation is still with the Jews of Israel. You think God is happy that the Jews in Israel deny His Son Our Lord Jesus Christ. Abraham, Isaac and Jacob would have been horrified if they knew that the Jews in Israel today were against Jesus Christ, the Messiah. Most probably Abraham's descendants have reached America. Of course, it is God's time and will, but as a faithful and devoted one, we are allowed to surmise that if any nation should be the Greatest Nation in our time, it is United States of America.

MAGA MAGA MAGA

Donald Trump had perhaps a past life like St. Paul and St. Augustine, but who is to judge. We are all sinners. Trump's father, Fred Trump had 48 years of deep friendship with Rabbi Wagner, a Polish Jew. Fred Trump donated land where the synagogue was built and contributed towards the construction. The son, Donald learned from his father how to be a faithful supporter of Israel and a generous friend of the Jews." Trump's daughter, Ivanka, converted to Judaism in accordance with Jewish law. The president himself has boasted on multiple occasions about "my Jewish grandchildren. "It is not a wonder Donald Trump possessing all the attributes of Joshua, successor of Moses that he could be a descendant of Ashkenazi Jew (see chapter 6) that is a descendant of Abraham and Jacob. If and when Donald J Trump is President and being probable a descendant of the tribe of Judah, God sees him as a great leader and how much pain, suffering and humiliation Trump went through. God did not say which nation He would bless, only to bless Abraham to make of him a great nation. God will bless Trump as precursor of God's Greatest Holy Nation or directly blesses Donald J Trump to lead God's Greatest Holy Nation and will curse those that dishonor him and God will bless all nations. That will be the fulfillment of Abraham's prophesies. America has come a long way to become a Superpower and with their leaders seeking the guidance of Jesus Christ to lead their country and people in a way of God's will. There was also a spiritual promise that all nations would be blessed through Jesus Christ, who was a descendant of Abraham (Matthew 1:1-16; Luke 3:23-34).

God's Greatest Holy Nation – United States of America.

As our Lord Jesus Christ says:

"Let not the authority of the writer deceive you whether it is little or great learning,
but let the love of pure truth lead you to read."
Source: Imitation of Christ

Copyright

Declaration

The decree of the Congregation for the Propagation of the Faith, A.A.S. 58, 1186 (approved by Pope Paul VI on October 14, 1966) states that the Nihil Obstat and Imprimatur are no longer required on publications that deal with private revelations, provided they contain nothing contrary to faith and morals. The author wishes to manifest unconditional submission to the final and official judgment of the Magisterium of the Church.

Prayers for the Rulers

O most Precious Blood of Jesus Christ, we honor, worship and adore You because of Your work of the everlasting covenant that brings peace to mankind. Heal the wounds in the most Sacred Heart of Jesus. Console the Almighty Father on His throne and wash away the sins of the whole world. May all revere You, O Precious Blood, have mercy. Amen.

Precious Blood of Jesus

Lord God, grant those in Government and Authority, health, peace, concord, and stability, so that they may exercise without offence the sovereignty that you have given them. Master, heavenly King of all ages, you give glory, honor, and power over the things of earth the sons of men. Direct Lord, their counsel, following what is pleasing and acceptable in your sight, so that by exercising with devotion and in peace and gentleness the power that You have given them, they may favor with You.

Pope Saint Clement I of Rome AD88 – AD97

First of all, then, I ask that supplications, prayers, petitions, and thanksgiving be offered for everyone, for kings and for all in authority, that we may lead a quiet and tranquil life in all devotions and dignity. This is good and pleasing to God our Savior, who wills everyone to be saved and come to knowledge of the truth.

Paul to Timothy 1,22:1-4

Acknowledgement

I am deeply grateful to my precious family, my wife Yoka, my daughter Carmen and her children Christian and Emma and the other daughter Jo-Ann and her husband Chris Hess and her children Brooklyn and Landan and my son Joey and his daughter Sunny and stepson Preston. I feel so blessed to have my brother Ralph Khoe as editor, my parishioner as well as minister from my Church Holy Family as editor and proofreader Carol Walsh and my valuable neighbor Thomas Tierney and lastly my publisher for my 7 beautiful Holy books, Editor Hazel Grace Thomson, Tyler Croman and Betsy Williams.

Introduction

My last book was Holy Family Exile to Egypt. That is what I said to myself. Well! As I kept praying, thoughts came into my mind, I did not think I was going to receive any inspiration about writing another book. Well! The inspiration came and I could not avoid, ignore or neglect the inspiration, it could be from Heaven. Obediently, I started writing and compiling the book to see if it is really from Heaven, sure enough I knew what to write. Firstly, I must know who Abraham's family and descendants were. To trace the lineage from 4124 years takes some research. The roadblock came with the birth of Jesus Christ. Holy Mother Mary and Saint Joseph had no descent except Jesus. Therefore, who were the descendants after Jesus. Since Jesus came from the line of Judah, and the line of Judah produced Moses, Joshua, King David, King Solomon, and Joseph lord of Pharaoh and ruler of all Egypt. It stands to reason that the tribe of Judah will keep on producing highly capable descendants.

Judah was the fourth son of Jacob and Leah. Moses was a descendant of Levi, the third son of Jacob and Leah. Moses should be known as a Levite. Levites were part of tribe of Judah. God chose Levi to be the patriarch of Israel's priesthood and temple caretakers called Levites (Exodus 6:16-20; Malachi 2:1, 4-6).

Various websites and books have a great deal of information connecting the 12 tribes of Israel to the nations of Western Europe and the United States today. Biblical, historical and archaeological evidence indicates that descendants of the so-called 10 lost tribes of ancient Israel migrated to northwestern Europe and the British Isles. It is more commonly understood that many peoples from these nations also settled in the United States and the Commonwealth nations such as Canada, Australia and New Zealand. For the above-noted reasons, we believe that the peoples who settled in northwestern Europe and the United States, Britain and the Commonwealth are largely the descendants of the 12 tribes of Israel today. The lost 10 tribes of ancient Israel include the Jewish population in the United States is estimated to be around 7.5 million people, or 2.4% of the total US population.

Former President Donald J Trump seem to possess the capabilities, the abilities and the knowledge to lead a nation. After all, he has demonstrated during his 4 years of presidency, there were no wars global or domestic, he had a great concern not only for his own family also for the country and the welfare of its people. What now is very remarkable at his age he perseveres in spite of the constant persecution and attempted assassination. His faith and love for God his family and country is evident. Possessing all these traits and characteristic, he could descent from the lineage of the tribe of Judah, he certainly could be a candidate to be a precursor of God's Greatest Holy Nation.

Dedication

To President Donald and Melania Trump

My first book was dedicated to President Donald and Melania Trump

And these are my holy books:

Holy Kings, Holy Queens, Holy Royalties

Holy Kings, Holy Queens, Holy Royalties Volume II

Super Holy Popes

Three Holy Kings

Holy Book Store

Holy Family Exile to Egypt

God's Greatest Holy Nation

By

Gaby Kool

CONTENTS

APPENDIX

Seeking the guidance of Jesus Christ to lead their country

People in a way of God's will.

Peace and Prosperity and Loyal Subjects for many years

Chapter 1

Abraham's Family

The Family of Abraham
Catholic Resource
by Felix Just, S.J., Ph.D.

Various biblical passages describe the *complex inter-relationships* in the family of Abraham (originally named Abram). Contrary to modern Western customs, it was acceptable in ancient times to marry close family relatives, including cousins and nieces. It was evidently also common for men to have more than one wife, and even to have children with women who were not their wives (slaves or concubines). For example, Abraham's first son was the child of his wife's slave-girl; and one biblical tradition even says that his wife, Sarah, was actually his half-sister. Similarly, the twelve sons of Jacob have four different mothers: the two wives of Jacob (who are his first cousins) and two other women (slave-girls of his wives).

A prominent feature of the biblical texts is also the *explanation of tribal origins* through various genealogies. Thus, the *Israelites* (the twelve tribes of Israel) see themselves as the descendants of the twelve sons of Jacob, son of Isaac, son of Abraham. In contrast, groups like the *Ishmaelites* and *Edomites* (to the south and southeast of the Israelites) are said to be descendants of Abraham's other children and grandchildren, while the neighboring *Moabites* and *Ammonites* (west of Israel) are described as descendants of Lot, Abraham's nephew.

Another important aspect of the biblical stories is what could be called *family rivalries and disputes*, esp. when younger sons usurp the inheritance rights of their older brothers. Thus, Abraham's inheritance is passed on to Isaac (not the first-born Ishmael), and then to Jacob (not his elder brother Esau).

Combining all the above points helps to explain both the close relationships and the bitter rivalries between the ancient Israelites and the neighboring

Semitic peoples. The Israelites (and modern Jews!) believe that the promises God made to Abraham (esp. that his descendants shall possess the Promised Land forever) were legitimately handed on to them through Isaac and Jacob (as described in the Bible), while the descendants of the other tribes (and modern Arabs!) believe that the land should belong to them, since they are descendants of the elder sons (and thus the rightful heirs) of Abraham.

The following charts can help us visualize some of these complex relationships:

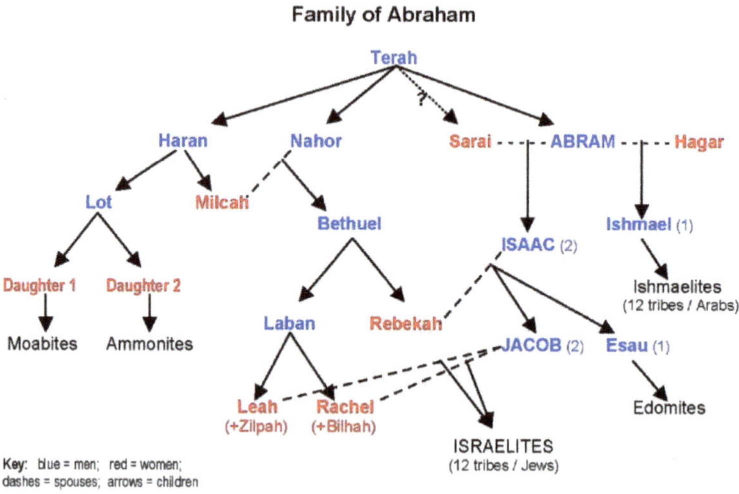

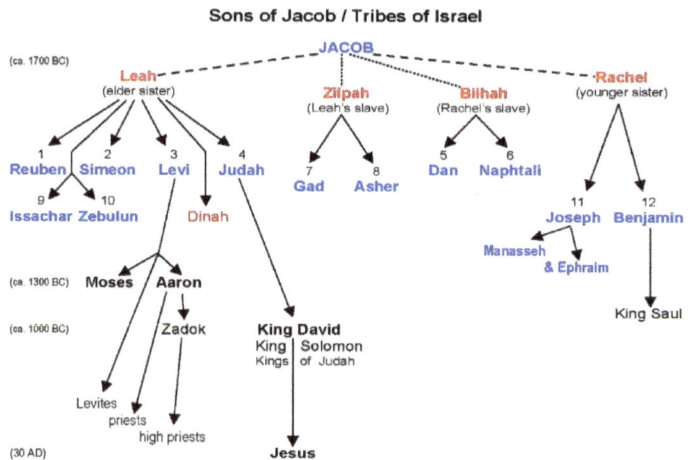

NOTES: (unless otherwise noted, all biblical references are from the **Book of Genesis**)

- **Terah**: from Ur of the Chaldeans; has three sons; wife not named (11:26-32; cf. Luke 3:34).
- **Haran:** dies in Ur before his father dies; wife not named; son Lot, daughters Milcah & Iscah (11:27-28).
- **Nahor:** marries Milcah, daughter of his brother Haran (11:29); have eight sons, incl. Bethuel (22:20-24).
- **Abram:** main character of Gen 12–25; recipient of God's promises; name changed to ABRAHAM (17:5); sons Ishmael (by Hagar) and Isaac (by Sarah); after Sarah's death, takes another wife, Keturah, who has six sons (25:1-4), including Midian, ancestor of the Midianites (37:28-36).
- **Lot:** son of Haran, thus nephew of Abram, who takes care of him (11:27–14:16; 18:17–19:29); wife and two daughters never named; widowed daughters sleep with their father and bear sons, who become ancestors of the Moabites and Ammonites (19:30-38).

Sarai: Abram's wife, thus Terah's daughter-in-law (11:29-31); Abram also calls her his "sister," which seems deceptive in one story (12:10-20); but in another story Abram insists she really is his half-sister (his father's daughter by another wife; 20:1-18); originally childless, but in old age has a son, Isaac (16:1–21:7); name changed to SARAH (17:15); dies and is buried in Hebron (23:1-20).

- Hagar: Sarah's Egyptian slave-girl; mother of Abram's first son, Ishmael; much conflict with Sarah after his birth; even more after the birth of Sarah's son, Isaac (16:1–21:21).
- Ishmael: first-born son of Abraham, by Hagar (16:1–17:27); wife or wives never named, but has 12 sons (25:12-16), the ancestors of 12 tribes of Ishmaelites (37:25-28). - *see below*
- Isaac: second son of Abraham, by wife Sarah, despite her old age (17:15-21; 21:1–35:29); marries Rebekah, who has twin sons, Esau & Jacob
- .Betheul: youngest son of Nahor & Milcah; wife unnamed; father of Rebekah (22:23) and Laban (24:29).
- Rebekah: daughter of Bethuel (22:23); becomes wife of Isaac (24:15–25:20); favors their younger son.

- Laban: son of Bethuel, brother of Rebekah; has extensive interactions with Jacob (24:29–31:55).
- Esau: elder twin son of Isaac & Rebekah (25:25); names of wives differ in two traditions (26:34 & 28:9 vs. 36:2-3); one is a daughter of Ishmael; his sons are ancestors of the Edomites (36:1-43).
- Jacob: younger twin son of Isaac & Rebekah (25:26); conflicts with Esau (25:27–27:46); marries Leah and Rachel, daughters of his uncle Laban (27:43–29:30); name changed to ISRAEL (32:28); has 12 sons (with two wives + two slave-girls), ancestors of the Israelites or "12 Tribes of Israel" (29:31–49:33). - *see below*
- Curiosity about the ages of the Patriarchs:
    - Abraham lived 175 years (Gen 25:7), which equals 7×5^2
    - Isaac lived 180 years (Gen 35:28), which equals 5×6^2
    - Jacob lived 147 years (Gen 47:28), which equals 3×7

The Bible says very little else about the "Twelve Tribes of Ismaelites" aside from naming the twelve sons of Ishmael in Gen 25:12-16 and again in 1 Chron 1:29-31.

- Gen 25:12-16 – "These are the descendants of Ishmael, Abraham's son, whom Hagar the Egyptian, Sarah's slave-girl, bore to Abraham./ These are the names of the sons of Ishmael, named in the order of their birth: Nebaioth, the firstborn of Ishmael; and Kedar, Adbeel, Mibsam, / Mishma, Dumah, Massa, / Hadad, Tema, Jetur, Naphish, and Kedemah. / These are the sons of Ishmael and these are their names, by their villages and by their encampments, twelve princes according to their tribes."
- 1 Chron 1:29-31 – "These are their genealogies: the firstborn of Ishmael, Nebaioth; and Kedar, Adbeel, Mibsam, / Mishma, Dumah, Massa, Hadad, Tema, / Jetur, Naphish, and Kedemah. These are the sons of Ishmael."
    - Adbeel, Massa, Kedemah - not mentioned anywhere else in the Bible
    - Mibsam & Mishma - not mentioned elsewhere, but different people with the same name appear in 1 Chron 4:25-26
    - Hadad - not mentioned elsewhere, but several other biblical characters are named Hadad, Ben-Hadad, Hadadezer, etc.
- Other biblical references to some of the sons of Ishmael (aside from Gen 25:12-16 and 1 Chr 1:29-31)

- o Nebaioth - also in Gen 28:9; 36:3; Isa 60:7
- o Kedar - also in Ps 120:5; Prov 21:4; Songs 1; Isa 21:16; 21:17; 42:11; 60:7; Jer 2:10; 49:28; Ezek 27:21
- o Dumah - also in Josh 15:52; Isa 21:11
- o Tema - also in Job 6:19; Isa 21:14; Jer 25:23
- o Jetur & Naphish - also in 1 Chron
- o The Hebrew Bible describes the "Twelve Tribes of Israel" as descendants of the twelve sons of Jacob (also named Israel), with four different mothers. The births of the *twelve sons* (and the significance of their names) are described in chronological order in the book of Genesis (29:31–30:24 & 35:16-20). The Bible contains several different listings of the twelve tribes. Each tribe has its own characteristics and eventually obtains its own territory:

- Reuben is the first-born son, and thus sometimes exercises a leadership role among his brothers; but he later loses favor and prominence.
- The tribe of Joseph (through his sons *Manasseh* and *Ephraim*) becomes the largest and most prominent by the time the Israelites enter the Promised Land and divide it among themselves.
- The tribe of Levi is uniquely important, not only because of Moses and Aaron, but since they become the *priestly tribe* (all the sons of Levi are priests, while members of any other tribe cannot be priests). The Levites do not receive a separate territory of their own, but rather live scattered among all the other tribes, where they serve as priests for the whole people.
- Although the first king of Israel (Saul) is from the tribe of Benjamin, the tribe of Judah becomes known as the *royal tribe*, due to the promise God makes to King David that his descendants will rule over Israel forever (2 Sam 7).

- Jacob's twelve sons are first mentioned in the order of their births, in Genesis 29:31–30:24 & 35:16-20.
  - o Leah (elder wife): 1) Reuben, 2) Simeon,
  - o 3) Levi, 4) Judah; later also 9) Issachar, 10) Zebulun
  - o Bilhah (Rachel's slave): 5) Dan, 6) Naphtali
  - o Zilpah (Leah's slave): 7) Gad, 8) Asher
  - o Rachel (younger wife): 11) Joseph, 12) Benjamin

- Manasseh & Ephraim – sons of Joseph, whose descendants figure prominently in the later history of Israel
- Moses and Aaron – leaders of the Israelites at the time of their migration out of Egypt and wandering in the Sinai desert. Page 5
- Kings David & Solomon – the two greatest rulers of the united Kingdom of Israel, from about 1100 to 930 BCE
- Tribe of Levi – becomes known as the "priestly tribe," since all cultic & temple officials had to belong to this tribe
- Tribe of Judah – becomes known as the "royal tribe," since all later Kings of Judah were descendants of King David

Why! How! Well, let us trace and track the lineage of the 12 tribes:

Reuben – Simeon – Levi – Judah – Dan – Naphtali – Gad – Asher – Issachar
Zebulun – Joseph – Benjamin

When God called Abraham, He promised him that because of his obedience, his descendants would become a great nation and that in him all nations of the earth would be blessed (Genesis 12:1-3). The physical blessings God gave Abraham would continue through his son Isaac and his grandson Jacob, also called Israel, whose 12 sons were the progenitors of the 12 tribes of Israel. There was also a spiritual promise that all nations would be blessed through Jesus Christ, who was a descendant of Abraham (Matthew 1:1-16; Luke 3:23-34).

Joshua: Successor to Moses, a military and great leader of Israel
Source: Encyclopedia Britannica

According to the biblical book named after him, Joshua was the personally appointed successor to Moses (Deuteronomy 31:1–8; 34:9) and a charismatic warrior who led Israel in the conquest of Canaan after the Exodus from Egypt. After sending spies into Canaan to report on the enemy's morale, Joshua led the Israelites in an invasion across the Jordan River. He took the important city of Jericho and then captured other towns in the north and south until most of Palestine was brought under Israelite control. He divided the conquered lands among the 12 tribes of Israel and then bade farewell to his people (Joshua 23), admonishing them to be loyal to the God of the covenant.

A careful reading of relevant biblical texts, stimulated by the study of external resources, has led scholars to a general agreement that Israel did not take Canaan by means of a single, comprehensive, calculated plan of conquest. It happened more gradually and more naturally, through progressive infiltration and acculturation. This relatively peaceful development, which went on for a couple of centuries, reached its fulfillment in the rise of David. Until then, for the most part, walled cities remained in Canaanite hands. Even if these cities were razed, as in the case of Hazor (Joshua 11), Israel does not seem to have made military use of them; David's occupation of Jerusalem was a first in this respect. The accounts of Joshua's campaigns (Joshua 10–11) seem to fit these realities; they are accounts of forays by a mobile community, moving ever westward, that increasingly constituted a force to be reckoned with in the open spaces between the walled cities.

Chapter 2

The 12 tribes of Israel divide into two kingdoms

After they spent time as slaves in Egypt, God delivered Abraham's descendants and allowed them to form the ancient nation of Israel. Over time, 10 of the tribes formed the northern kingdom of Israel and two of the tribes formed the southern kingdom of Judah. Due to their breaking of His laws, God allowed the northern kingdom to be taken captive by the Assyrians and, later, the southern kingdom to be taken by the Babylonians.

After 70 years, many of the captives of Judah returned to Jerusalem and rebuilt the city. Because of this and their renewed diligence in keeping God's Sabbath, their history continued. However, the northern 10 tribes largely disappeared from history. As a result, they are sometimes referred to as the lost 10 tribes of Israel. But while their nation disappeared, the descendants of these people continued to exist.

To follow the history of the 12 tribes of Israel after the fall of their nation to the Assyrians in 721 B.C., we must recognize the path of their deportation and identify them by the names given them by their conquerors. Various websites and books have a great deal of information connecting the 12 tribes of Israel to the nations of Western Europe and the United States today, and it would be impossible to cover all this material in this answer. But here is some of the documentation.

When the Assyrians conquered Samaria, the capital of the northern kingdom, they transported many of the Israelites "to Assyria, and placed them in Halah and by the Habor, the River of Gozan, and in the cities of the Medes" (2 Kings 17:6). Shortly after the Israelites came into these lands, scholars note the appearance of peoples in this area called Cimmerians and Scythians. The Assyrians also called them Khumri, Ghomri, Gimiri (derivatives of King Omri of Israel) and Iskuza (derivative of Isaac).

The famous Black Obelisk in the British Museum includes a pictorial etching of King Jehu of Israel bowing and paying tribute to King Shalmaneser of Assyria. The text speaks of Jehu, son (really a successor) of Omri, giving the Assyrian king silver, gold, a golden bowl, a golden vase, golden tumblers, golden buckets, tin, a staff and spears. This was the time during which Israel paid tribute to Assyria as a vassal nation prior to rebelling and being destroyed by Assyria.

As Israelites disappear, Scythians and Cimmerians appear

Historian Tamara Rice writes: "The Scythians did not become a recognizable national entity much before the eighth century B.C. By the seventh century B.C. they had established themselves firmly in southern Russia. And analogous tribes, possibly even related clans, though politically entirely distinct and independent, were also centered on the Altai [Mountains of southern Russia and Mongolia] Assyrian documents place their appearance there in the time of King Sargon (722-705 B.C.), a date which closely co0rresponds with that of the establishment of the first group of Scythians in southern Russia" (The Scythians, 1961, pp. 19-20, 44).

Boris Piotrovsky in his book From the Lands of the Scythians notes, "Two groups, Cimmerians and Scythians, seem to be referred to in Urartean and Assyrian texts, but it is not always clear whether the terms indicate two distinct peoples or simply mounted nomads. Beginning in the second half of the eighth century B.C, Assyrian sources refer to nomads identified as the Cimmerians; other Assyrian sources say these people were present in the land of the Mannai and in Cappadocia for a hundred years, and record their advances into Asia Minor and Egypt.

"The Assyrians used Cimmerians in their army as mercenaries; a legal document of 679 B.C. refers to an Assyrian 'commander of the Cimmerian regiment'; but in other Assyrian documents they are called 'the seed of runaways who know neither vows to the gods nor oaths'" (1975, pp. 15, 18).

The Bible likewise indicates that the ancient Israelites would eventually migrate in a northwesterly direction away from Jerusalem. According to a prophecy yet to be fulfilled, God's Servant will "restore the preserved ones of Israel" (Isaiah 49:6), and these peoples will come from "the north and the west" back to Jerusalem (verse 12). While it is certainly clear that displaced

Israelites were among these peoples, we should also note that not all Scythians or Cimmerians were Israelites. "Scythian" does not necessarily refer to a specific ethnic group. But it did include Israelites, who later moved in a northwesterly direction into Europe following their collapse as a nation.

Historians link the Cimmerians with the Gauls or Celts of northwest Europe Historian Samuel Lysons linked some of the people who populated northwest Europe with these Cimmerians. As he put it, the Cimmerians seemed "to be the same people with the Gauls or Celts under a different name."

English historian and scholar George Rawlinson wrote: "We have reasonable grounds for regarding the Gimirri, or Cimmerians, who first appeared on the confines of Assyria and Media in the seventh century B.C., and the Sacae of the Behistun Rock, nearly two centuries later, as identical with the Beth-Khumree of Samaria, or the Ten Tribes of the House of Israel" (noted in his translation of History of Herodotus, Book VII, p. 378.

Danish linguistic scholar Anne Kristensen concurs, stating: "There is scarcely reason, any longer, to doubt the exciting and verily astonishing assertion propounded by the students of the Ten Tribes that the Israelites deported from Bit Humria, of the House of 'Omri, are identical with the Gimirraja of the Assyrian sources. Everything indicates that Israelite deportees did not vanish from the picture but that, abroad, under new conditions, they continued to leave their mark on history" (Who Were the Cimmerians, and Where Did They Come From? Sargon II, the Cimmerians, and Rusa I, translated from the Danish by Jørgen Læssøe, The Royal Danish Academy of Sciences and Letters, No. 57, 1988, pp. 126-127).

The Cimmerians were an ancient people who lived north of the Caucasus and the Sea of Azov. They were driven out of southern Russia by the Scythians in the late 8th century BC and moved into Anatolia. The Cimmerians were an Iranic people who shared a common language, culture, and origins with the Scythians. However, they were distinct political entities from the Scythians, even though they were archaeologically indistinguishable. The Cimmerians may have originally lived in southern Ukraine, where the Crimea is still named after them. Archaeologists have identified them with the Novocerkassk culture, which lived on the grass plains between the river Prut and the Lower Don from about 900–650 BC.

The Bible likewise indicates that the ancient Israelites would eventually migrate in a northwesterly direction away from Jerusalem. According to a prophecy yet to be fulfilled, God's Servant will "restore the preserved ones of Israel" (Isaiah 49:6), and these peoples will come from "the north and the west" back to Jerusalem (verse 12).

Archaeological evidence tracing the travels of the 12 tribes of Israel

In addition to historical evidence, Scythian burial grounds have indicated a connection between these peoples and those of Nordic ancestry. For many years, scholars believed the Scythians were Mongols because groups of these nomadic people moved east, but the discovery of art and even a frozen corpse of a Scythian warrior indicate otherwise.

In July 2006 in the Altai Mountains of Mongolia near China and Russia, scientists made a rare find. German scientists who were part of the discovery team reported that the extremely well-preserved mummy of a Scythian warrior was that of "a 30-to 40year-old man with blond hair" ("Ancient Mummy Found in Mongolia," Spiegel Online International, Aug. 25, 2006). Blond hair, of course, is a characteristic of Europeans not Mongols. Prior to the discovery of this mummy, art obtained from numerous Scythian burial grounds had likewise indicated that these peoples were related to Europeans rather than Mongols. Because Scythian chiefs were buried with all their collected wealth, including wives, horses and art, detailed images of Scythians, their clothes and weapons have been uncovered. These discoveries depict their men with long, flowing locks, facial hair and Caucasian features.

Biblical, historical and archaeological evidence indicates that descendants of the so-called 10 lost tribes of ancient Israel migrated to northwestern Europe and the British Isles. It is more commonly understood that many peoples from these nations also settled in the United States and the Commonwealth nations such as Canada, Australia and New Zealand. For the above-noted reasons, we believe that the peoples who settled in northwestern Europe and the United States, Britain and the Commonwealth are largely the descendants of the 12 tribes of Israel today. The lost 10 tribes of ancient Israel include the Jewish population in the United States is estimated to be around 7.5 million people, or 2.4% of the total US population.

God's faithfulness in blessing the descendants of the ancient Israelites will continue after Christ's return and the establishment of the Kingdom of God here on earth. As Jesus

explained to His apostles: "Assuredly I say to you, that in the regeneration, when the Son of Man sits on the throne of His glory, you who have followed Me will also sit on twelve thrones, judging the twelve tribes of Israel" (Matthew 19:28). Even New Jerusalem will have 12 gates named after the 12 tribes of Israel (Revelation 21:12).

Is it true, as the ecumenicists claim, that "we (Christians, Jews, and Muslims) are all Abraham's children"? Yes and no. It's true formally that all three religions lay claim to a direct lineage to Abraham. In a formal sense, then, it is true, but in the material sense it is not true.

The Jews in our Lord's time neglected this duty. They shut their eyes against events occurring in their own day of the most significant character. They refused to see that prophecies were being fulfilled around those who were bound up with the coming of Messiah and that Messiah Himself was with them. But still, the eyes of the Jews were blinded. They still obstinately refused to believe that Jesus was the Christ. And hence they drew from our Lord the question, "How is it that you do not discern this time?" God's faithfulness in blessing the descendants of the ancient Israelites will continue after Christ's return and the establishment of the Kingdom of God here on earth. As Jesus explained to His apostles:

"Assuredly I say to you, that in the regeneration, when the Son of Man sits on the throne of His glory, you who have followed Me will also sit on twelve thrones, judging the twelve tribes of Israel" (Matthew 19:28). Even New Jerusalem will have 12 gates named after the 12 tribes of Israel (Revelation 21:12)

Source: The Editors of Encyclopedia Britannica

Cimmerian people

Cimmerian, member of an ancient people living north of the Caucasus and the Sea of Azov, driven by the Scythians out of southern Russia, over the Caucasus, and into Anatolia toward the end of the 8th century BC. Ancient writers sometimes confused them with the Scythians. Most scholars now believe that the Cimmerians assaulted Urartu (Armenia) about 714 BC, but in 705, after being repulsed by Sargon II of Assyria, they turned aside into Anatolia and in 696–695 conquered Phrygia. In 652, after taking Sardis, the capital of Lydia, they reached the summit of their power. Their decline soon began, and their final defeat may be dated from 637 or 626, when they were routed by Alyattes of Lydia. Thereafter, they were no longer mentioned in historical sources but probably settled in Cappadocia, as its Armenian name, Gamir, suggests.

The origin of the Cimmerians is obscure. Linguistically they are usually regarded as Thracian or as Iranian, or at least to have had an Iranian ruling class. They probably did live in the area north of the Black Sea, but attempts to define their original homeland more precisely by archaeological means, or even to fix the date of their expulsion from their country by the Scythians, have not so far been completely successful. One theory identifies them with what is known to archaeologists as the "Catacomb" culture. This culture was ousted from southern Russia by the "Srubna" culture advancing from beyond the Volga just as the Cimmerians were ousted by the invading Scythians, but that upheaval took place in the second half of the 2nd millennium BC, and a gap of several centuries separates it from the appearance of historic Cimmerians in Asia. Some authorities identify them with "Thraco-Cimmerian" remains of the 8th–7th century BC found in the southwestern Ukraine and in central Europe; these may perhaps be looked upon as traces of the western branch of the Cimmerians, who, under fresh Scythian pressure, eventually invaded the Hungarian plain and survived there until about 500 BC.

Chapter 3
Judah and Benjamin

The descendants of two of the 12 tribes of Israel are the Jewish people and the Bene Ephraim, also known as Telugu Jews:

- Judah and Benjamin

These two tribes survived the destruction of most of the other tribes and allowed their descendants to return to their homeland after the Babylonian Exile. The tribe of Judah is known as the Tribe of Kings and is symbolized by a lion, which represents strength, leadership, and royal dignity. The tribe of Benjamin provided Israel with its first king, Saul, and later became part of the tribe of Judah.

- Ephraim

The Bene Ephraim, or Telugu Jews, claim descent from the tribe of Ephraim. They say they traveled from Israel to southern India over 1,000 years ago, and have practiced their own oral traditions and customs since then.

Other groups that claim descent from the tribes of Israel include:

- Druze: Some speculate that the Druze are descended from the tribe of Zevulun.

- Ethiopian Jews: Also known as Beta Israel, these Jews claim descent from the tribes of Dan, Gad, Asher, and Naphtali.

- Bnei Menashe: Also known as Mizo Jews, these people claim descent from the tribe of Manasseh.

- Samaritans: Some of their adherents claim descent from the tribe of Manasseh.

Judah, one of the 12 tribes of Israel, descended from Judah, who was the fourth son born to Jacob and his first wife, Leah. It is disputed whether the name Judah was originally that of the tribe or the territory it occupied and which was transposed from which.

After the Israelites took possession of the Promised Land, each was assigned a section of land by Joshua, who had replaced Moses as leader after the latter's death. The tribe of Judah settled in the region south of Jerusalem and in time became the most powerful and most important tribe. Not only did it produce the great kings David and Solomon but also, it was prophesied, the Messiah would come from among its members. Modern Jews, moreover, trace their lineage to the tribes of Judah and Benjamin (absorbed by Judah) or to the tribe, or group, of clans of religious functionaries known as Levites. This situation was brought about by the Assyrian conquest of the Kingdom of Israel in 721 BC, which led to the partial dispersion of the 10 northern tribes and their gradual assimilation by other peoples. (Legends thus refer to them as the Ten Lost Tribes of Israel.)

- Judah, Biblical eponymous ancestor of the tribe
- Perez, his son
- Caleb, military leader from the time of the Exodus, and his brother Kenaz
- Othniel, leader from the period of the judges and son of Kenaz
- 0Boaz, Obed, and Jesse, the great-grandfather, grandfather and father, respectively, of King David
- David, king of Israel and founder of the Davidic line
- The kings of Judah, all of whom were descended from David
- The prophets Amos, Habakkuk, Isaiah, Jeremiah, Joel, Micah, Obadiah, Zechariah, and Zephaniah
- Shealtiel and Zerubabel, figures of the Babylonian Exile
- Nehemiah, governor of Judea under the Persian Empire
- The Exilarchs and the great teachers of the House of Hillel
- Jesus Christ, according to the genealogy of Matthew 1:1

Saint Joachim, the son of Barpathir, was of the tribe of Judah, and was a descendant of King David, to whom God had revealed that the Savior of the world would be born from his seed. Saint Anna was the daughter of Matthan the priest, who was of the tribe of Levi. Saint Anna's family came from Bethlehem.Sep 9, 2021.

Chapter 4

Tribe of Judah

New World Encyclopedia

Map of the tribal allotments (c. 1759 C.E.); Judah is to the far south

The Tribe of Judah (Hebrew Yəhuda, "Praise") is one of the Hebrew tribes, founded by Judah, son of Jacob. The tribe was allotted the southernmost area of Canaan after the territory's conquest by the Israelites under Joshua. It became both the most powerful and the most important of the tribes. The religion centered on the Jewish God Yahweh first took roots among the people of Judah. From this tribe came the great kings David and Solomon and all of the kings recognized by the Bible as good. The Messiah, as a lineal descendant of David, also comes from the tribe of Judah.

Together with the Tribe of Benjamin and elements of the Tribe of Levi, the descendants of Judah eventually formed the southern Kingdom of Judah in the ancient land of Israel. The Judahites were not among the "lost" ten tribes of the northern Kingdom of Israel when it fell to the Assyrians in 722 B.C.E. Instead, the people of Judah were exiled to Babylon about 586, but were eventually able to return and rebuild their nation. In time, the tribe of Judah became identified with the entire Hebrew nation and gave its name to the people known today as the Jews.

Contents

- 1 In the Bible
- o Origins
- o Exodus and Conquest
- o Period of Judges
- o The "United" Kingdom
- o Legacy
- Notable members
- References

- Credits
- The lion is the symbol of the Tribe of Judah, as depicted in this sculpture outside a synagogue The tribe of Judah descended from the patriarch Judah, the fourth son of Jacob and Leah (Gen. 29:35). Judah's daughter-in-law Tamar played a pivotal role in ensuring the survival of Judah's lineage, giving birth to the twins Peres and Zerah. Later, Judah and his sons went down with Jacob into Ancient Egypt (Gen. 46:12; Ex. 1:2). On his deathbed, Jacob prophesied that Judah would be the leader and ruler of his brothers:

Judah, your brothers will praise you;
your hand will be on the neck of your enemies;
your father's sons will bow down to you.
You are a lion's cub, O Judah...
The scepter will not depart from Judah,
nor the ruler's staff from between his feet,
until he comes to whom it belongs
and the obedience of the nations is his. (Gen. 49:8-10)

Exodus and Conquest

By the time of the Exodus, the tribe of Judah had reportedly increased to the number of 74,000 males (Num. 1:26, 27). The clans which then composed the tribe are said to have been the Shelanites, Perizzites, Zerahites, Hezronites, and Hamulites (Num. 26:19-22). Judah marched at the front rank on the east side of the Tabernacle (Num. 2:3-9; 10:14); its standard, as is supposed, being a lion's whelp.

"The second lot came out for the tribe of Simeon... Their inheritance lay within the territory of Judah" (Josh. 19:1)

Caleb, the son of Jephunneh, represented the tribe as one of the twelve spies sent to gather intelligence in Canaan (Josh. 13:6; 34:19), being the only one other than Joshua to deliver a faithful report. Under Caleb, during the wars of conquest, Judah conquered that portion of the country which was later assigned to it as its inheritance (Josh. 14:6-15; 15:13-19).

Judah's inheritance was at first fully one-third of the whole country west of the Jordan River, in all about 2,300 square miles (Josh. 15). However, a later distribution gave Simeon about one thousand square miles out of the portion of Judah (Josh. 19:9). That which remained to Judah was still very large in proportion to the inheritance of the other tribes.

The boundaries of the territory are described in the Joshua 15:20-63. It is said to have extended south as far as Kadesh Barnea, about 50 miles south of Beersheba, and west as far as Gaza, Ashdod, and Ekron. This allotted Judah a territory that included lands and fortified cities still under control of the Philistines, Jebusites, and other Canaanite peoples, with whom they would struggle for centuries.

Period of Judges: The tribe of Judah is said to have been the first tribe to successfully attack the Canaanites after the death of Joshua. However, its triumphs described in the first chapter of the Book of Judges—including victories over the Philistinecities of Gaza, Ashdod, and Ekron as well as the Jebusite city of Jerusalem—appear to be either exaggerated or short-lived. The Philistine strongholds and Jerusalem remained uncaptured, and Judges 15 describes a situation in which the men of Judah admit that "the Philistines are rulers over us."

From the Judges 1:16 it is learned that the non-Israelite people known as the Kenites united with Judah and apparently became a clan of the tribe. Some scholars speculate that something similar may have happened with some of the other clans of Judah, particularly the Perizzites. The Bible usually lists this people as a Canaanite tribe against whom Israel must fight (Gen. 3:8 and 15:19, etc.), but Numbers 26:20 identifies them as part of the tribe of Judah through his son Perez. Thus the Perizzites may have actually joined Judah in Canaan and later were "adopted" into Judah's origin-story. Judges 1:4 may hint at the moment when it states that "Lord gave the Canaanites and Perizzites into their hands and they struck down ten thousand men at Bezek."

Judah is not mentioned in the song of Deborah (Judges 5) among the tribes who joined in that war against Canaanite forces. Nor does Judah appear to have cooperated in any of the exploits of the judges except its own member, Othniel. On the other hand, Judah joined with its Philistine overlords in the attempt to capture the judge Samson, a member of the tribe of Dan (Judges

15). However, Judah did support the other tribes and took the lead in punishing the tribe of Benjamin for its sin with regard to the affair of the Levite's concubine (Judges 18-19).

In the accounts of the kingdom of Saul, Judah is given a distinct identity from the other tribes (1 Sam. 17:52, 18:16). After Saul's death, David established a separate Kingdom of Judah (2 Sam. 2:1) while the northern tribes remained loyal to the house of Saul under his heir, Ish-bosheth. After seven and one-half years, with the defeat of Ish-bosheth, Judah and Israel were united under David's kingship. Although several rebellions arose, this union continued for 80 years, through the reign of King Solomon. After the division of Judah and Israel under Rehoboam and Jeroboam I respectively, the history of the tribe of Judah becomes fused with that of the Kingdom of Judah itself. The tribe of Benjamin, together with a considerable portion of the priestly Levite tribe attending to duties in the Temple of Jerusalem, joined Judah in this nation. It is especially noteworthy that the prophetic movement of Yahwism took root in the territory of Judah. It became at times the state religion of that kingdom, and formed the basis for the religion later known as Judaism.

While the northern tribes were effectively scattered and "lost" after the Assyrian conquest of the Kingdom of Israel in 722 B.C.E., the Judahites were able to maintain their ethnic and cultural identity after being exiled to Babylon under Nebuchadrezzar II of Babylon in 587. Under Cyrus the Great of Persia, many returned to Jerusalem, rebuilt the Temple and established a national identity as "Jews" which has lasted until this day. The northern tribes reconstituted to some degree in Samaria, but were denigrated by the Jews for intermarrying with foreign peoples and for worshiping outside of Jerusalem at Mount Gerizim. What remained of the northern tribes either evolved into the Samaritans, assimilated with Judah as "Jews," or were simply considered to be "lost.

Nearly all Jews today consider themselves as descendants of the tribe of Judah. Some do claim membership in the Levites, the priestly clan that—like other Jews—was exiled to Babylon and returned to rebuild the Temple. However, Jews with family names such as Levy (Levi), Rubin (Reuben), Simon (Simeon), Benjamin, Asher, etc. are unable to document their genealogies as going back to these historical tribes

Notable members

- Judah, Biblical eponymous ancestor of the tribe.
- Perez, his son.
- Caleb, military leader from the time of the Exodus, and his brother Kenaz.
- Othniel, leader from the period of the judges and son of Kenaz.
- Boaz, Obed, and Jesse, the great-grandfather, grandfather and father, respectively, of King David.
- David, king of Israel and founder of the Davidic line.
- The kings of Judah, all of whom were descended from David.
- The prophets Amos, Habakkuk, Isaiah, Jeremiah, Joel, Micah, Obadiah, Zechariah, and Zephaniah.
- Shealtiel and Zerubabel, figures of the Babylonian Exile.
- Nehemiah, governor of Judea under the Persian Empire.
- The Exilarchs and the great teachers of the House of Hillel.
- Jesus Christ, according to the genealogy of Matthew 1:1.

BOOK OF 1 CHRONICLES
The Genealogy of the Sons of Judah

1 Chronicles 2:3-55

The sons of Judah *were* Er, Onan, and Shelah. *These* three were born to him by the daughter of Shua, the Canaanitess. Er, the firstborn of Judah, was wicked in the sight of the Lord; so He killed him. And Tamar, his daughter-in-law, bore him Perez and Zerah. All the sons of Judah *were* five.

The sons of Perez *were* Hezron and Hamul. The sons of Zerah *were* Zimri, Ethan, Heman, Calcol, and Dara—five of them in all.

The son of Carmi *was* Achar, the troubler of Israel, who transgressed in the 0accursed thing.

The son of Ethan *was* Azariah.

Also the sons of Hezron who were born to him were Jerahmeel, Ram, and Chelubai. Ram begot Amminadab, and Amminadab begot Nahshon, leader of the children of Judah; Nahshon begot Salma, and Salma begot Boaz; Boaz begot Obed, and Obed begot Jesse; Jesse begot Eliab his firstborn, Abinadab the second, Shimea the third, Nethanel the fourth, Raddai the fifth, ¹⁵ Ozem the sixth, *and* David the seventh.

Now their sisters *were* Zeruiah and Abigail. And the sons of Zeruiah *were* Abishai, Joab, and Asahel—three. ¹⁷ Abigail bore Amasa; and the father of Amasa *was* Jether the Ishmaelite.

Caleb the son of Hezron had children by Azubah, *his* wife, and by Jerioth. Now these were her sons: Jesher, Shobab, and Ardon. When Azubah died, Caleb took Ephrath as his wife, who bore him, Hur. And Hur begot Uri, and Uri begot Bezalel.

Now afterward Hezron went in to the daughter of Machir the father of Gilead, whom he married when he *was* sixty years old; and she bore him Segub. Segub begot Jair, who had twenty-three cities in the land of Gilead. (Geshur and Syria took from them the towns of Jair, with Kenath and its towns—sixty towns.) All these *belonged to* the sons of Machir the father of Gilead. After Hezron died in Caleb Ephrathah, Hezron's wife Abijah bore him Ashhur the father of Tekoa.

The sons of Jerahmeel, the firstborn of Hezron, *were* Ram, the firstborn, and Bunah, Oren, Ozem, *and* Ahijah. Jerahmeel had another wife, whose name was Atarah; she was the mother of Onam. The sons of Ram, the firstborn of Jerahmeel, were Maaz, Jamin, and Eker. The sons of Onam were Shammai and Jada. The sons of Shammai *were* Nadab and Abishur.

And the name of the wife of Abishur *was* Abihail, and she bore him Ahban and Molid. The sons of Nadab *were* Seled and Appaim; Seled died without children. The son of Appaim *was* Ishi, the son of Ishi *was* Sheshan, and Sheshan's son *was* Ahlai. The sons of Jada, the brother of Shammai, *were* Jether and Jonathan; Jether died without children. The sons of Jonathan *were* Peleth and Zaza. These were the sons of Jerahmee

Now Sheshan had no sons, only daughters. And Sheshan had an Egyptian servant whose name *was* Jarha. Sheshan gave his daughter to Jarha his servant as wife, and she bore him Attai. Attai begot Nathan, and Nathan begot Zabad; Zabad begot Ephlal, and Ephlal begot Obed; Obed begot Jehu, and Jehu begot Azariah; Azariah begot Helez, and Helez begot Eleasah; Eleasah begot Sismai, and Sismai begot Shallum; Shallum begot Jekamiah, and Jekamiah begot Elishama.

The descendants of Caleb the brother of Jerahmeel *were* Mesha, his firstborn, who was the father of Ziph, and the sons of Mareshah the father of Hebron. The sons of Hebron *were* Korah, Tappuah, Rekem, and Shema. Shema begot Raham the father of Jorkoam, and Rekem begot Shammai. And the son of Shammai *was* Maon, and Maon *was* the father of Beth Zur.

Ephah, Caleb's concubine, bore Haran, Moza, and Gazez; and Haran begot Gazez. And the sons of Jahdai *were* Regem, Jotham, Geshan, Pelet, Ephah, and Shaaph.

Maachah, Caleb's concubine, bore Sheber and Tirhanah. She also bore Shaaph the father of Madmannah, Sheva the father of Machbenah and the father of Gibea. And the daughter of Caleb *was* Achsah.

These were the descendants of Caleb: The sons of Hur, the firstborn of Ephrathah, *were* Shobal the father of Kirjath Jearim, Salma the father of Bethlehem, *and* Hareph the father of Beth Gader. And Shobal the father of Kirjath Jearim had descendants: Haroeh, *and* half of the *families of* Manuhoth. The families of Kirjath Jearim *were* the Ithrites, the Puthites, the Shumathites, and the Mishraites. From these came the Zorathites and the Eshtaolites.

The sons of Salma *were* Bethlehem, the Netophathites, Atroth Beth Joab, half of the Manahethites, and the Zorites.

And the families of the scribes who dwelt at Jabez *were* the Tirathites, the Shimeathites, *and* the Suchathites. These *were* the Kenites who came from Hammath, the father of the house of Rechab.

2:3–4. The details of the sordid story (Gen. 38) of Judah's sons, two of whom (Er and Onan) were slain by the Lord and the third (Shelah) withheld from Tamar, are not discussed here. The chronicler wanted to introduce the two sons of Judah (Perez and Zerah) in order to follow the line through Perez to the Davidic family.

2. genealogies of perez and zerah (2:5–8)

2:5–8. These verses mention only selective and representative descendants (sons often means descendants of later generations) of Perez and Zerah as is clear from the fact that Achar (or Achan) is here noted as the son of Carmi (v. 7) and Carmi's father is not mentioned at all. Perhaps Zimri (v. 6) is a variant spelling of Zabdi because in the story of Achan's sin (Josh. 7) Achan was a son of Carmi, who was a son of Zabdi (Josh. 7:1, marg.), son of Zerah. Even so, the period from Zerah (born ca. 1877 b.c.) to Achan (an adult in 1406, Josh. 7) was almost 500 years, much too long for four generations. The chronicler's reference to Zerah, then, is primarily to introduce Ethan, Heman, Calcol, and Darda (Dara in most Heb. mss.; cf. marg.), all actually the sons of Mahol, whose ancestor was Zerah (cf. comments on 1 Kings 4:31), and celebrated sages to whom Solomon was compared (1 Kings 4:31; Ps. 89, title.

2:9–20. The chosen line now continues through Hezron, son of Perez, Judah's son. In line with Ruth 4:18–21, the descent goes on to David (1 Chron. 2:9–15; see the chart "David's Ancestry from Abraham" near 1 Sam. 16:1–13). The lineage also includes David's immediate family and half-sisters (1 Chron. 2:16–17; see the chart "David's Family" near 2 Sam. 3:2–5). Caleb, another son of Hezron, was not the Caleb who was Joshua's associate. (In 1 Chron. 2:9 the Heb. has "Kelubai"; cf. marg., a variant spelling of Caleb; cf. v. 42.) His lineage follows in verses 18–20 and is expanded later in verses 42–55. Segub, another son of Hezron, was born of the daughter of Makir, a son of Manasseh (Gen. 50:23) and father of Gilead (Num. 26:29). The name of Gilead was given the upper

Transjordan district. The incident of the taking of 60 Gilead towns by Geshur and Aram (areas northeast of Gilead) is otherwise unknown in the

Old Testament. Another son, born posthumously to Hezron by his wife Abijah, was Ashhur.

2:25–41. The oldest son of **Hezron, Jerahmeel** (cf. v. 9), is mentioned last. His family descent appears only here, though Jerahmeelites were viewed as a clan closely related to Judah in David's time (1 Sam. 27:10).

4.	Genealogy of caleb (2:42–55): 2:42–55. The line of Caleb, Hezron's third son (cf. v. 9), introduced briefly in verses 18–20, is expanded here. Many of these names appear elsewhere as place-names (e.g., Ziph, Josh. 15:24; Mareshah, Josh. 15:44; Hebron, Josh. 15:54; Tappuah, Josh. 15:34; Rekem, Josh. 18:27; Shema, Josh. 15:26; etc.). This does not prove a connection, but since most of these places lay in Judah, they were probably founded by the various Calebites listed here.

Of particular interest are the references to Bethlehem (1 Chron. 2:51, 54), birthplace of both David and Jesus. The town was founded by or named after the great-grandson of Caleb through Caleb's wife Ephrathah (v. 50, spelled Ephrath in v. 19). The combination of Bethlehem and Ephrathah appears also in the story of Rachel's death in childbirth (Gen. 35:19), where it is used anachronistically; in Ruth 4:11 in reference to blessing on Ruth; and in Micah 5:2 with respect to the birth of the Messiah.

Chapter 5
Birth of the Child Jesus

I saw Joseph on the following day arranging a seat and couch for Mary in the so-called Suckling Cave of Abraham, which was also the sepulcher of Maraha, his nurse. It was more spacious than the cave of the Crib. Mary remained there some hours, while Joseph was making the latter more habitable. He brought also from the city many different little vessels and some dried fruits. Mary told him that the birth hour of the Child would arrive on the coming night. It was then nine months since her conception by the Holy Ghost. She begged him to do all in his power that they might receive as honorably as possible this Child promised by God, this Child supernaturally conceived; and she invited him to unite with her in prayer for those hard-hearted people who would afford Him no place of shelter. Joseph proposed to bring some pious women whom he knew in Bethlehem to her assistance; but Mary would not allow it, she declared that she had no need of anyone. It was five o'clock in the evening when Joseph brought Mary back again to the Crib Cave. He hung up several more lamps, and made a place under the shed before the door for the little she-ass, which came joyfully hurrying from the fields to meet them.

When Mary told Joseph that her time was drawing near and that he should now betake himself to prayer, he left her and turned toward his sleeping place to do her bidding. Before entering his little recess, he looked back once toward that part of the cave where Mary knelt upon her couch in prayer, her back to him, her face toward the east. He saw the cave filled with the light that streamed from Mary, for she was entirely enveloped as if by flames. It was as if he were, like Moses, looking into the burning bush. He sank prostrate to the ground in prayer, and looked not back again. The glory around Mary became brighter and brighter, the lamps that Joseph had lit were no longer to be seen. Mary knelt, her flowing white robe spread out before her. At the twelfth hour, her prayer became ecstatic, and I saw her raised so far above the ground that one could see it beneath her. Her hands were crossed upon her breast, and the light around her grew even more resplendent. I no longer saw the roof of the cave.

Above Mary stretched a pathway of light up to Heaven, in which pathway it seemed as if one light came forth from another, as if one figure dissolved into another, and from these different spheres of light other heavenly figures issued. Mary continued in prayer, her eyes bent low upon the ground. At that moment she gave birth to the Infant Jesus. I saw Him like a tiny, shining Child, lying on the rug at her knees, and brighter far than all the other brilliancy. He seemed to grow before my eyes. But dazzled by the glittering and flashing of light, I know not whether I really saw that, or how I saw it. Even inanimate nature seemed stirred. The stones of the rocky floor and the walls of the cave were glimmering and sparkling, as if instinct with life. Mary's ecstasy lasted some moments longer. Then I saw her spread a cover over the Child, but she did not yet take Him up, nor even touch Him. After a long time, I saw the Child stirring and heard Him crying, and then only did Mary seem to recover full consciousness. She lifted the Child, along with the cover that she had thrown over it, to her breast and sat veiled, herself and Child quite enveloped. I think she was suckling Him. I saw angels around her in human form prostrate on their faces.

It may, perhaps, have been an hour after the birth when Mary called St. Joseph, who still lay prostrate in prayer. When he approached, he fell on his knees, his face to the ground, in a transport of joy, devotion, and humility. Mary again urged him to look upon the Sacred Gift from Heaven, and then did Joseph take the Child into his arms. And now the Blessed Virgin swathed the Child in red and over that in a white veil up as far as under the little arms, and the upper part of the body from the armpits to the head, she wrapped up in another piece of linen. She had only four swaddling cloths with her. She laid the Child in the Crib, which had been filled with rushes and fine moss over which was spread a cover that hung down at the sides. The Crib stood over the stone trough, and at this spot the ground stretched straight and level as far as the passage, where it made a broader flexure toward the south. The floor of this part of the cave lay somewhat deeper than where the Child was born, and down to it steps had been formed in the earth. When Mary laid the Child in the Crib, both she and Joseph stood by Him in tears, singing the praises of God.

Chapter 6
The Destruction of the Second Temple in 70 AD

Following the destruction of the Second Temple in Jerusalem in 70 AD, the majority of Jews were forced to flee Judea, leading to a widespread dispersal across the Roman Empire known as the Jewish Diaspora, with many being sold into slavery by the Romans; they settled in various regions around the Mediterranean, including Mesopotamia, Egypt, and North Africa, as they were unable to live in Jerusalem which was renamed Aelia Capitolina by the Romans and largely prohibited to Jews.

Following the destruction of the Second Temple in Jerusalem by the Romans in 70 AD, most Jews dispersed throughout the Roman Empire, leading to what is known as the Jewish Diaspora, settling in regions like Mesopotamia (modern Iraq), the Mediterranean lands of southern Europe, North Africa, and parts of Asia Minor, including present-day Turkey, Greece, and Egypt; essentially scattering across various areas around the Mediterranean basin. Key points about the Jewish Diaspora after the Temple's destruction:

- Large-scale displacement:

  A significant portion of the Jewish population was either killed or exiled from Judea following the Roman siege of Jerusalem.

- Areas of settlement:

  Jews settled in regions like Mesopotamia, Egypt, Greece, Italy, Spain, and later, Northern Europe. During the Middle Ages, due to increasing migration and resettlement, Jews divided into distinct regional groups that today are generally addressed according to two primary geographical groupings: the Ashkenazi of Northern and Eastern Europe, and the Sephardic Jews of Iberia (Spain and Portugal), North Africa and the Middle East. These groups have parallel histories sharing many cultural similarities as well as a series of massacres, persecutions and expulsions, such as the expulsion from England in 1290, the expulsion from Spain in 1492, and the expulsion from Arab countries in 1948–1973. Although the two branches comprise many unique ethno-cultural practices and have links to their local host populations (such as Central Europeans for the Ashkenazim and Hispanics and Arabs for the Sephardim), their shared religion and ancestry, as well as their continuous communication and population transfers, has been responsible for a unified sense of cultural and religious Jewish identity between Sephardim and Ashkenazim from the late Roman period to the present.

Source: Wikipedia

How many years was Noah before Abraham?

The whole sum of the years are 1656. From the said flood of Noah, unto Abraham's departing from Chaldea, were 422years and ten days. For the said flood continued one whole year and ten days.

Apparently, yes, the Ashkenazi Jews are (part of) the Tribe of Judah (which is the source of the word "Jew", in Hebrew "יהודה" is the Tribe of Judah and "יהודי" is Jewish) and the Tribe of Binyamin (those two tribes were not exiled with the rest of Bnei Yisrael)

Who are the Ashkenazi descended from?

About half of Jewish people around the world today identify as Ashkenazi, meaning that they descend from Jews who lived in Central or Eastern Europe. The term was initially used to define a distinct cultural group of Jews who settled in the 10th century in the Rhineland in western Germany.Nov 30, 2020. Like other Jewish ethnic groups, the Ashkenazi originate from the Israelites and Hebrews of historical Israel and Judah. Ashkenazi Jews share a significant amount of ancestry with other Jewish populations and derive their ancestry mostly from populations in the Middle East, Southern Europe and Eastern Europe.

Ashkenazi Jews are descended from Jews who lived in Central and Eastern Europe, including Germany, Poland, and Russia. The term "Ashkenazi" was originally used to describe a cultural group of Jews who settled in the Rhineland in western Germany in the 10th century. The largest study to date of ancient DNA from Jewish individuals reveals unexpected genetic subgroups in medieval Germen Ashkenazi Jews and sheds light on the "founder event" in which a small population gave rise to most present-day Ashkenazi.

About half of Jewish people around the world today identify as Ashkenazi, meaning that they descend from Jews who lived in Central or Eastern Europe. The term was initially used to define a distinct cultural group of Jews who settled in the 10th century in the Rhineland in Western Germany.

Related Stories

Ancient DNA Reveals Asian Ancestry Introduced to East Africa in Early Modern Times

Findings clarify and complicate understanding of Swahili history. Despite much speculation, many gaps exist in our understanding of the origin of Ashkenazi Jews and the demographic upheavals they experienced during the second millennium.

To answer some of these pressing questions, the 30-person team — led by Shai Carmi at The Hebrew University and David Reich at HMS — analyzed DNA from the remains of 33 individuals buried in a medieval Jewish cemetery in Erfurt, Germany.

Erfurt's medieval Jewish community existed between the 11th and 15th centuries, with a short gap following a massacre in 1349. At times, it thrived and was one of the largest Jewish communities in Germany. Following the expulsion of all Jews in 1454, the city built a granary on top of the Jewish cemetery.

In 2013, the granary stood empty and the city permitted its conversion into a parking lot. This required additional construction and an archaeological rescue excavation. The genetics team received a special permit from the local Jewish community, which allowed the researchers to retrieve DNA from detached teeth that had already been collected as part of the rescue excavation.

The analysis revealed two distinct subgroups within the remains: one with greater Middle Eastern ancestry, which may represent Jews with origins in Western Germany, and another with greater Eastern and Central European ancestry. The modern Ashkenazi population formed as a mix of these groups and absorbed little to no outside genetic influences over the 600 years that followed, the authors said.

Some disease-causing mutations that are widespread in modern Ashkenazi Jews are suspected to have been introduced by members of the founding group long ago. The team found some of these mutations in Erfurt as well, indicating that the medieval Ashkenazi population indeed originated from an extremely small set of founders.

Further evidence came from mitochondrial DNA, which is part of the genome transmitted only from mothers. Analyses showed that one third of the Erfurt individuals descended in their maternal line from a single ancestral woman, again highlighting how small the founding population must have been, the authors said.

Despite the insights it provides, the study was limited to one cemetery and one time period. The researchers hope it will pave the way for future analyses of samples from other sites, including those from antiquity, to continue unraveling the complexities of Jewish history.

Source: Havard Medical School

Source: Wikipedia

The history of the Jews in Germany goes back at least to the year 321 CE, and continued through the Early Middle Ages (5th to 10th centuries CE) and High Middle Ages (*circa* 1000–1299 CE) when Jewish immigrants founded the Ashkenazi Jewish community. The community survived under Charlemagne, but suffered during the Crusades. Accusations of well poisoning during the Black Death (1346–53) led to mass slaughter of

German Jews, while others fled in large numbers to Poland. The Jewish communities of the cities of Mainz, Speyer and Worms became the center of Jewish life during medieval times. "This was a golden age as area bishops protected the Jews, resulting in increased trade and prosperity."

During the 13th century, Jews across Europe faced increasing persecution and expulsion from many countries, particularly in England where King Edward I expelled the entire Jewish population in 1290 due to growing antisemitism and resentment towards their role as moneylenders; this trend continued with other European nations expelling Jews in the following decades.

Why were the Jews expelled from England in 1290?

In 1290, the gradual deterioration of Christian-Jewish relations in England came to a head when King Edward could only secure parliament's grant of further taxation of his people to aid his war with France by making sacrifices. The expulsion of the Jews was the price he agreed to pay.

Herbert D. Katz Center

Though the Jewish Middle Ages was a time of persecutions and expulsions, it was as much a time of creativity and vibrancy in Judaism—from the proliferation of mystical (kabbalistic) texts and the composition of beautiful rhymed poems to the growth of scientific and medical knowledge and the appearance of new forms of piety. The fellowship year devoted intense study to this complex century, one in which the experience of medieval Jews was deeply entangled with that of Christians and Muslims. Fellows brought expertise about Judaism, Christianity, and Islam, and this intellectual cross-semination was as exciting as it was fruitful. Projects ranged from the image of the Jew in legends of the Virgin Mary to the Jewish curriculum, childrearing and women's practices, and the attitudes of Jews to war and worship. Methodologically, the scholars found ways to engage their materials and questions cooperatively from a range of intellectual perspectives and approaches, from intellectual to social history.

Elisheva Baumgarten, Ruth Mazo Karras, and Katelyn Mesler edited the year's volume, it is called Entangled Histories Knowledge, Authority, and Jewish Culture in the Thirteenth Century (2016).

How many Jewish people died in the Holocaust between 1933-1945?

Holocaust Encyclopedia

In total, six million Jewish men, women, and children were murdered by the Nazi German regime and its allies and collaborators. This genocide is now known as the Holocaust. Antisemitism was at the foundation of the Holocaust. Antisemitism, the hatred of or prejudice against Jews, was a basic tenet of Nazi ideology. This prejudice was also widespread throughout Europe.

During the Holocaust, the Nazis and their allies and collaborators murdered Jews in many places using several methods. The two main methods of murder were poison gas and mass shootings. They also murdered Jews in other acts of violence and by deliberately denying them access to adequate food, shelter, medical care, and other necessities.

Council of Europe

The Holocaust was one of the reasons why the Council of Europe was set up in 1949, just four years after the liberation of Auschwitz-Birkenau. The aim was to prevent such a genocide happening again in Europe, and to ensure that human life and human rights would be respected, page 26 no matter what the person's nationality, ethnicity, race, religion or sexual orientation. Within its wider role of promoting and protecting human rights, democracy and the rule of law, the Council of Europe works to combat anti-Semitism, homophobia and anti-gypsyism, and to promote the rights of Roma and the disabled.

THE DECLARATION OF THE ESTABLISHMENT OF THE STATE OF ISRAEL Ministry of Foreign affairs – GOV. II

On May 14, 1948, on the day in which the British Mandate over a Palestine expired, the Jewish People's Council gathered at the Tel Aviv Museum, and approved the following proclamation, declaring the establishment of the State of Israel. The new state was recognized that night by the United States and three days later by the USSR.

ERETZ-ISRAEL [(Hebrew) - the Land of Israel, Palestine] was the birthplace of the Jewish people. Here their spiritual, religious and political identity was shaped. Here they first attained to statehood, created cultural values of national and universal significance and gave to the world the eternal Book of Books.

After being forcibly exiled from their land, the people kept faith with it throughout their Dispersion and never ceased to pray and hope for their return to it and for the restoration in it of their political freedom. Impelled by this historic and traditional attachment, Jews strove in every successive generation to re-establish themselves in their ancient homeland. In recent decades they returned in their masses. Pioneers, ma'pilim [(Hebrew) - immigrants coming to Eretz-Israel in defiance of restrictive legislation] and defenders, they made deserts bloom, revived the Hebrew language, built villages and towns, and created a thriving community controlling its own economy and culture, loving peace but knowing how to defend itself, bringing the blessings of progress to all the country's inhabitants, and aspiring towards independent nationhood.

In the year 5657 (1897), at the summons of the spiritual father of the Jewish State, Theodore Herzl, the First Zionist Congress convened and proclaimed the right of the Jewish people to national rebirth in its own country.

This right was recognized in the Balfour Declaration of the 2nd November, 1917, and re-affirmed in the Mandate of the League of Nations which, in particular, gave international sanction to the historic connection between the Jewish people and Eretz-Israel and to the right of the Jewish people to rebuild its National Home.

The catastrophe which recently befell the Jewish people - the massacre of millions of Jews in Europe - was another clear demonstration of the urgency of solving the problem of its homelessness by re-establishing in Eretz-Israel the Jewish State, which would open the gates of the homeland wide to every Jew and confer upon the Jewish people the status of a fully privileged member of the comity of nations.

Survivors of the Nazi holocaust in Europe, as well as Jews from other parts of the world, continued to migrate to Eretz-Israel, undaunted by difficulties, restrictions and dangers, and never ceased to assert their right to a life of dignity, freedom and honest toil in their national homeland.

In the Second World War, the Jewish community of this country contributed its full share to the struggle of the freedom- and peace-loving nations against the forces of Nazi wickedness and, by the blood of its soldiers and its war effort, gained the right to be reckoned among the peoples who founded the United Nations.

On the 29th November, 1947, the United Nations General Assembly passed a resolution calling for the establishment of a Jewish State in Eretz-Israel; the General Assembly required the inhabitants of Eretz-Israel to take such steps as were necessary on their part for the implementation of that resolution. This recognition by the United Nations of the right of the Jewish people to establish their State is irrevocable. This right is the natural right of the Jewish people to be masters of their own fate, like all other nations, in their own sovereign State.

Chapter 7
The Trump Family's Immigrant Story

BY: NATASHA FROST – SEPTEMBER 14, 2023

For decades, they denied their German roots, claiming to be of Scandinavian origin.

He had been a sickly child, unsuited to hard labor, and feared the effects of the draft. It might have been illegal, but America didn't care about this law-breaking—at that time, Germans were seen as highly desirable migrants—and Trump was welcomed with open arms. Less than two weeks later, he arrived in New York, where he would eventually make a small fortune. More than a century later, his grandson, Donald Trump, became the 45th president of Friedrich's adopted home.

But for decades, Trump denied this German heritage altogether, instead claiming that his grandfather's roots lay further north, in Scandinavia. "[He] came here from Sweden as a child," Trump asserted in his co-written book The Art of the Deal. In fact, his cousin and family historian John Walter told The New York Times, Trump maintained the ruse at the request of his own realtor father, Fred Trump, who had obfuscated his German ancestry to avoid upsetting Jewish friends and clients. "After the war," Walter told the *Times*, "he's still Swedish. [The lie] was just going, going, going."

Trump is the son, and grandson, of immigrants: German on his father's side, and Scottish on his mother's. None of his grandparents, and only one of his parents, was born in the United States or spoke English as their mother tongue. (His mother's parents, from the remote Scottish Outer Hebrides, lived in a majority Gaelic-speaking community.)

Friedrich and Elizabeth Trump, Colorized by Marina Amaral

Friedrich Trump came to the United States amid a flood of Germans that year alone, an estimated 1 million made the journey to settle in America. It was, the *Times* reported, "the start of an adventurous life as a barber, restaurateur, saloonkeeper, hotelier, entrepreneur, gold rush prospector, shipwreck survivor and New York real-estate investor."

He married a woman from his German hometown, Kallstadt, where his parents had owned vineyards, and attempted to return home with his fortune. But when his draft dodging came to the fore, the couple lost their Bavarian citizenship and were obliged to return to America for good. There, they had three children: Trump's father, Fred, was the middle child. Born in the Bronx borough of New York City in 1905, Fred Trump was an all-American child who spoke no German. Later, he would become one of the city's most successful young businessmen, amassing a fortune even as many around him slumped into financial ruin.

In the mid-1930s, a young Fred Trump went to a party "dressed in a fine suit and sporting his trademark moustache." Two Scottish sisters were at that same party in Queens: The younger one, Mary Anne MacLeod, was a domestic worker considering a return to her island homeland. "Something clicked between the maid and the mogul," write Michael Kranish and Marc Fisher in their biography *Trump Revealed*. When Trump returned that night to the home he shared with his mother, the authors continued, he made an announcement: He had met the woman he planned to marry.

Fred and Mary Trump, parents of Donald Trump

MacLeod might have been living in poverty in the United States, but her origins were even less palatable. She was the child of a fisherman and subsistence farmer, and the last in a family of 10 children born in the village of Tong on the Scottish Isle of Lewis. "It was not an easy existence," reports *Politico*. This vast Gaelic-speaking family lived together in a modest gray pebble-dash house, "surrounded by a landscape of properties local historians and genealogists characterized with terms like 'human wretchedness' and 'indescribably filthy.'"

Married to Fred Trump, MacLeod lived a radically different life of fur coats and 50-foot yachts. In 1942, she became an American citizen and returned only occasionally to her native Scotland, where her son now owns multiple properties. While Friedrich Trump had had moderate success in real estate, he died unexpectedly in a flu pandemic before his 50th birthday, and so did not live to see many of his projects come to fruition. At his death, his net worth was around $510,000 in present-day dollars. Under the Elizabeth Trump & Son moniker, Fred Trump and his mother Elizabeth continued this work, and turned it into a flourishing business.

Trump's international origins make him relatively unusual among American presidents. Of the last 10 presidents, only two—Trump and Barack Obama—have had a parent born outside of the United States. Trump's own immediate family has been similarly international: Two of his three
wives were naturalized American citizens, originally from the Czech Republic and Slovenia. Only one of his five children, Tiffany, is the child of two American-born citizens, while his daughter, Ivanka, is the first Jewish member of the First Family in American history. But so far as his biographers have been able to tell, none of his international roots extends to Sweden.

By: Natasha Frost – September 14, 2023

**Fred and Donald Trump's Jewish connection
BY Ariel Kahana**

In the 1950s, Fred Trump, the president's late father, donated the plot of land where the Beach Haven Jewish Center was built in Brooklyn and contributed towards its construction. He affectionately referred to Rabbi Israel Wagner, who approached the elder Trump for help, as "My Rabbi."

Published on 10-16-2020 12:30.

Donald Trump, left, with his father, Fred, in 1987 | File photo: Getty Images

Over the past few days, a story has spread in Jewish American circles about the roots of the Trump family's ties to New York city's religious Jews. According to the story, Rabbi Israel Wagner, a Holocaust survivor, began organizing prayer *minyan* (quora) in the underground parking garage in the apartment building he lived in Brooklyn, which was built in 1950 and mostly housed fellow survivors. As the years passed, these *minyans* expanded "exponentially."

"Having only heard about their landlord, Mr. Fred Trump, by name, Rabbi Wagner set out to meet him in the hopes that Mr. Trump would assist them in establishing a new facility as a Jewish community center," said the message being disseminated on Jewish WhatsApp groups in the US, parts of which were originally posted on the Beach Haven Jewish Center's website.

"From the first meeting, a deep friendship sparked between Mr. Trump, a Lutheran land developer, and Rabbi Wagner, a Polish Jew. Their mutual love, respect, and friendship only deepened over the next 48 years. Mr. Fred Trump donated the plot of land where the synagogue was built and contributed towards the construction. He then attended the dinner every year and generously donated to the Beach Haven Jewish Center. He affectionately referred to Rabbi Wagner as 'My Rabbi' at their yearly meetings," the website said.

The message goes on: "The apartment owner continued giving financial assistance to the synagogue over the years. He was a Christian person who instilled his respect for Jews in his 14-year-old son, a wild and adventurous boy. Today, the rabbi's son clearly remembers seeing the boy at the laundromat, while he and his friends were praying the shacharit (morning prayer). The building owner taught his son the importance of responsibility. His name was Fred Trump and the boy's name was Donald Trump. As we all know, the son learned from his father how to be a faithful supporter of Israel and a generous friend of the Jews."

A confidant of President Trump confirmed the story to *Israel Hayom.* Although Trump is broadly accused by leftist circles in the US of being anti-Semitic, it appears that even in his childhood he was raised with an affinity toward the Jews. As a reminder, many years later, Trump's daughter, Ivanka, converted to Judaism in accordance with Jewish law. The president himself has boasted on multiple occasions about "my Jewish grandchildren."

Source: Israel Hayom's daily newsletter and never miss our top stories

Letter to Catholics for Catholics
Catholics for Catholics, Phoenix, Arizona
Donald J Trump

July 30, 2024

Catholics for Catholics, Phoenix, Arizona

Melania and I are grateful for your continued support and encouragement. Your love of country is evident in everything you do. We admire your dedication to preserving America's founding principles through your faith.

You have realized God's Grace and righteousness by continuing to seek and share His wisdom. Through His love, you have imparted hope, healing, and fellowship during life's most meaningful moments and milestones. You should take great pride in upholding the sacred Catholic values of love, compassion, and charity.

May God continue to bless you all.

Sincerely,

Donald J Trump

Source: AP- Associated Press

Evangelical leaders, she said, are pushing this idea that, "this is God's man, and we can't ask why. We don't have to ask why. It doesn't matter if he's moral, it doesn't matter if he's religious. It doesn't matter if he lies compulsively. It's for the greater good that we get him re-elected."

At the Republican National Convention, Arkansas Gov. Sarah Huckabee Sanders, a conservative Christian and Trump's former White House press secretary, invoked God when she addressed the first assassination attempt against him.

"God Almighty intervened because America is one nation under God, and he is certainly not finished with President Trump," she said. "And our country is better for it."

Anthea Butler, professor of religious studies at the University of Pennsylvania, said white evangelicals likely see him as instrumental to their goals, such as his appointment of conservative, anti-abortion justices to the Supreme Court.

Source: Catholic Exchange: Patrick O'Hearn – First Attempt Trump assassination

During President Donald Trump's tenure, a statue of Our Lady of Fatima was placed in the White House. The statue was a gift from Fr. Andrew Mahana, a Maronite priest, who also exorcised the White House on January 20, 2017 (inauguration night), according to an article by Catholic. A friend of mine who worked for President Trump said that they referred to the west wing of the White House as the "West Wing Chapel" due to the Marian statue and other religious items.

On May 13, 1981, Pope St. John Paul II survived an assassination attempt. That day was the feast of Our Lady of Fatima, and Pope St. John Paul II himself credited his survival to Our Lady of Fatima. The pope said, "The gunman fired the gun, but Mary guided the bullet;"[2] another source stated the pope's words as, "One hand shot, and other guided the bullet."[3] Exactly one year after being shot, the pope visited the apparition site of Fatima. He placed the bullet in Mary's crown, saying, "You saved me, you saved me."

Our Lady of Fatima appeared to three children, St. Jacinta, St. Francisco, and Ven. Sister Lucia, on the 13th of every month from May to October of 1917 in Fatima, Portugal—each time asking for prayer and penance. Most significantly, however, on **July 13, 1917**, Our Lady of Fatima revealed the three secrets, including the vision of hell to the children—a most important apparition.

**On Saturday, July 13, 2024, President Trump survived first assassination
attempt in Butler, PA.**

This was the 107th anniversary of Our Lady's appearance at Fatima. This last July 13th fell on a Saturday—a day which Catholics honor Mary especially. July 13th is *also* the feast day of Rosa Mystica, one of Mary's titles and a recently approved Marian apparition. Furthermore, one mile away from the grounds on which Trump's rally was held sits a Catholic Church with a grotto to Our Lady of Fatima—a grotto that we think was facing President Trump at the time.

I believe Our Lady of Fatima saved President Donald Trump's life. She guided the bullets away from him just as she did for Pope St. John Paul II. Our Lady is God's instrument. She plays a special intercessory role to Our Lord, and it was her intercession that helped spare President Trump's life. Certainly, the prayers of Fr. Jason Charron, a Ukrainian Catholic pastor who gave the benediction before the rally, called down heavenly protection.

Interestingly, President Trump was shot at 6:11 pm EST, which, as someone pointed out to me, could refer to Ephesians 6:11: "Put on the whole armor of God, that you may be able to stand against the wiles of the devil." President Trump later credited God for saving his life after the attack: "It was God alone who prevented the unthinkable from happening." Indeed,

God's armor was surrounding President Trump, especially that of His Mother.

Second attempt assassination at Trump

Talking about Trump being persecuted only it appears today September 15, 2024, there was an attempted assassination at Trump Internation Golf Club in West Palm Bech, Florida. The suspect name is Ryan Westly Routh. This was the second attempt on the life of former President Donald J Trump. Not a random guy with an AK-47, suspect is in custody. Trump was 300-500 yards away from suspect. Trump praises the Secret Service for acting quickly. Trump is fine. Suspect had Gopro Camera in his backpack

By Karl Vick – Time – September 23, 2024 – 2:57 pm EDT
Third attempt at killing Donald Trump

Asif Merchant was arrested on July 12. He had just loaded his luggage into his ride to the airport, commencing a journey either to his wife and children in Iran or to a different wife and children in his native Pakistan. In weeks of secretly recorded conversations with a federal informant, Merchant had confided that he had families in both countries. He also, according to an FBI affidavit, said he had come to America to arrange the assassination of "a political person."

The identity of that person was not explicitly stated, either by Merchant or by his handler in Iran's Islamic Revolutionary Guard Corps, according to a leaked document that was posted online by U.S. Sen. Charles Grassley on Sept. 5 after, the Iowa Republican said, it was provided to him by a whistleblower. But, along with other evidence, the documents all but confirm that Donald Trump was the person Merchant was authorized to offer up to $1 million to kill.

Trump receives scapular & relic of the True Cross from a Carmelite priest at NYC rally September 19, 2024 by Catholics for Catholics

In an unexpected turn following one of his largest rallies in New York City, former President Donald Trump reportedly paused backstage to pray with a Carmelite priest who presented him with a religious scapular and a relic of the True Cross. The Carmelite priest laid his hands on Trump and felt an electric charge through his hands to Donald Trump. The Carmelite priest spoke to Ron Ray about it. The incident, which unfolded moments after Trump exited the stage, has quickly become a topic of fascination among his supporters and detractors alike, with the religious symbolism further fueling discussions around Trump's appeal to Christian conservatives.

The rally, held in New York City, was billed as one of Trump's most significant public appearances, drawing large crowds of enthusiastic supporters. While the focus of the event was primarily political, it is the alleged post-rally encounter with the priest that has captured public attention. According to reports, the Carmelite priest approached Trump after his speech, offering prayers and presenting him with two sacred objects—a scapular, a traditional Catholic devotional item, and what was described as a relic of the True Cross, an artifact believed by some to be a fragment of the cross upon which Jesus Christ was crucified.

The gesture is said to have resonated with Trump, whose political base includes a significant number of evangelical Christians and conservative Catholics. His public expressions of faith, particularly during his presidency, were a key aspect of his outreach to religious voters. This moment, if verified, could further strengthen his bond with religious communities who view him as a defender of their values.

Relics of the True Cross are considered among the most sacred objects in Christian tradition, with many believing they hold great spiritual significance. The offering of such a relic to Trump is notable, as it underscores the strong religious undertones of his political persona and the support he garners from certain religious groups. The scapular, often associated with the Carmelite order, is worn as a sign of devotion and protection, adding another layer of religious symbolism to the encounter.

The reported prayer session and gifting of sacred objects have sparked curiosity about the former president's relationship with the priest and whether it was a planned encounter or a spontaneous act of faith. While the Carmelite order is known for its deep-rooted spiritual traditions, including the wearing of scapulars as a form of devotion to the Virgin Mary, the public nature of the event raises questions about its broader significance, particularly as Trump positions himself for a possible 2024 presidential run.

Critics of Trump have questioned the authenticity of the event, suggesting that it may have been staged to appeal to religious voters ahead of the upcoming election cycle. Meanwhile, his supporters view the moment as further evidence of Trump's commitment to faith and religious freedom, key issues that have defined much of his political identity.

As with many aspects of Trump's political life, the story has quickly divided opinion, with some praising the former president for his openness to religious expressions and others casting doubt on the authenticity of the claims. The lack of independent verification from neutral sources has left many wondering whether this latest narrative will become a significant part of Trump's ongoing political journey.

Chapter 8
Conversion of a Jew

Source: Roy Schoeman

Saul wanted to destroy the church, Saul accepted the task of crushing the Christian movement. On his journey to Damascus, a light from the sky suddenly flashed around him. He fell to the ground and heard a voice saying to him, 'Saul, Saul, why are you persecuting me? Saul asked "Who are you, sir? The reply came, "I am Jesus, whom you are persecuting." Roy Schoeman like the former Saul, also a passionate and ardent believer of Judaism encountered a similar mystical experience. He was baptized into the Catholic Church in 1992 and since then has been evangelizing to share his Catholic Faith.

According to Roy Schoeman, Salvation comes from the Jews. Jesus was a Jew, his Mother was a Jew, His apostles were all Jews. God has chosen the Jews to be His people. Why?

- Because He could have chosen other nations at random, and it could be any nation.
- Margaret Mary Alacoque asked Jesus in a vision, "Why have you chosen me? Jesus replied: "Because, there is no one more worthless and insignificant than you."

• Another reason is that when Abraham was told to kill his son. Abraham instantly obeyed.

The Jews have played their part well even if they were a few of them, they have evangelized and spread the Gospel throughout the world. All the apostles were willing to die for Christ and all were martyred except St. John. After Jesus surrenders His Spirit to the Father and dies, an earthquake started which destroyed the Temple and rips the veil covering the Holy of Holies, and so ended the role of Judaism (end of sacrificing animals). In 70 AD the Jews lost their country when the Romans destroyed the Temple completely, and actual destruction of Jerusalem and so began the wandering Jews in different country until 1967 when the Jews returned to Israel. Sadly, the Jews were persecuted for nearly 2000 years. There were the antisemitic. There were those who accuse them of killing Jesus.

Source: Carolyn Salomons

However, in 1463 Cardinal Juan de Torquemada said" No other race was more dignified, more noble, saintlier and more religious" than that of the Jewish people. Torquemada did not believe Jews enjoyed any biological superiority to other people, but he understood they had a unique spiritual heritage which set them apart. Today, we can say, "Have any people survived as long as the Jews without a homeland? Was ever it known that a nation wandered the earth for nearly 2000 years and yet retained their glorious heritage? This almost defies explanation. Time and time again in history when people lose their land they lose their identity. Not so the Jews, and the achievement is more than survival. For despite all the enmities and persecutions levelled against the Jews, despite even diabolical attempts to wipe them from the face of the earth, the Jews have not only survived, not only prospered, not only flourished, but they have regained their homeland. Not just any land, but their ancestral land, Israel.

Source: Cardinal Juan de Torquemada Judaism and the Catholic Church are not two different religions. They are one and the same religion. Evidence points strongly that the Catholic Church is the continuation and fulfillment of Judaism. One example, there were many miracles, prophesies and prophets in the Old Testament. That ended when Jesus was crucified and died. Now, which religion manifests all these miracles and prophesies. The Catholic church has many scientific evidences, such as Lourdes, Fatima, La Salette, Medjugorje and so on……. But, because the Catholic Church has the Fullness of the Faith, God supplements this faith with an abundance of spiritual experiences. Not only priests and nuns enjoy these experiences, but also lay people, go to any Catholic Church and ask some of the faithful if they had encountered any spiritual experiences, and they will be happy to relate their experiences, although some priests are reluctant or do not accept or want to hear any private revelations.

In my 15 years as a Catholic Book Store owner, I have listened to many private revelations, whether it is true or not. Unfortunately, I am not taught or trained to discern private revelations. But, most people are shy or fear that a priest would reject their experiences. Most priests do not want to hear private revelations. If priest rejects private revelation, who can discern whether it is true or not. We understand that clergy are not taught or trained in their seminaries about private revelations, perhaps now, it is prudent and useful to train them during their formation. Certainly, the days to come and in the future as a sign of the time warrant discernment is absolutely necessary. If the revelations are true, then sharing their experience is a powerful tool for evangelization.

Imagine if the Catholic priests did not believe Rabbi Israel Zolli who had a vision of Christ appearing to him and said to him, "You are here for the last time; from now on, you will follow Me." Rabbi Israel would not be baptized and became a Catholic priest. Today only a trickle of Jews would be converted. Today, Jews are converted to Catholicism, mostly after they have received a revelation from our Lord Jesus or Blessed Mother Mary. Now, they believe the Messiah is Jesus and when He died and resurrected Jesus made sure that His apostles all Jews continues to build His Church. Actually, the Jews do not need to be converted, they just transit from Judaism to Catholic because Catholicism is a continuation from Judaism.

Source: Holy Kings, Holy Queens, Holy Royalties Volume II

September 2023: Well! The story of Pharisees continues, as God said in Genesis "They are people of stiff-neck and hard-hearted, they still want to continue with their persecution of Jesus. Members of Torah Judaism Knesset: Moshe Gaffney and Yakov Asher 2 members of Israeli Prime Minister Benjamine Netanyahu's administration have proposed a bill that whoever mentioned or talks about Jesus will be persecuted and go to jail.

The Pharisees have not stopped persecuting Jesus. After 2000 years they still harbor a lot of hate for Jesus. Why? As God says they are a nation of stiff-necked and hard-hearted people. That is why they still bear a grudge especially after they have been exiled for 2000 years and experienced the horrible Holocaust. Following the proposal from Members of Torah October 7, 2023 Hamas attacked Israel. It is a long war, it is still continuing whilst I am writing and compiling this book, 9/16/2024.
Noticing the signs of the time:

The Jews in our Lord's time neglected this duty. They shut their eyes against events occurring in their own day of the most significant character. They refused to see that prophecies were being fulfilled around those who were bound up with the coming of Messiah and that Messiah Himself was with them. But still, the eyes of the Jews were blinded. They still obstinately refused to believe that Jesus was the Christ. And hence they drew from our Lord the question, "How is it that you do not discern this time?"

In John 6:53–57, Jesus says, "Very truly I tell you, unless you eat the flesh of the Son of Man and drink his blood, you have no life in you. Whoever eats my flesh and drinks my blood has eternal life, and I will raise them up at the last day. For my flesh is real food and my blood is real drink. Whoever eats my flesh and drinks my blood remains in me, and I in them. Just as the living Father sent me and I live because of the Father, so the one who feeds on me will live because of me. This is the bread that came down from heaven. Your ancestors ate manna and died, but whoever feeds on this bread will live forever." Upon hearing these words, many of Jesus' followers said, "This is a hard teaching" (verse 60), and many of them actually stopped following Him that day (verse 66).

Gospel - John 3:16-21

God so loved the world that he gave his only-begotten Son, so that everyone who believes in him might not perish but might have eternal life. For God did not send his Son into the world to condemn the world, but that the world might be saved through him. Whoever believes in him will not be condemned, but whoever does not believe has already been condemned, because he has not believed in the name of the only-begotten Son of God. And this is the verdict, that the light came into the world, but people preferred darkness to light, because their works were evil. For everyone who does wicked things hates the light and does not come toward the light, so that his works might not be exposed. But whoever lives the truth comes to the light, so that his works may be clearly seen as done in God.

The first part of today's gospel episode (Jn 3:16-18) beautifully presents the summary of the identity, the mission and the Character of Jesus Christ. The second part of the passage (Jn 3:19-21) explains why the world rejected Jesus even after the glorious revelation of his divine identity through his resurrection.

Appendix

In America 235,151,203 Christian believe in Christ whilst 7,208.000 of Jews from Israel deny Christ. If the Jews do not recognize Jesus Christ as our God and Messiah, how can they be blessed as God's Greatest Nation.

Source: Google

As of December 2023, the Jewish population in Israel was approximately 7,208,000, or 73.2% of the country's total population. This includes about 503,000 Jews who live outside of Israel's borders in the West Bank.

The Jewish population in the United States is estimated to be around 7.5 million people, or 2.4% of the total US population, as of 2020.

According to the USCCB, there are 71,128,395 Catholics in the United States, which is around 22% of the population. The Catholic Church has been the largest religious body in the United States for over a century.

According to a 2023 Gallup poll, 68% of Americans identify as Christian, which is the largest religious group in the country. This includes 33% Protestant, 22% Catholic, and 13% other Christian denominations.

As of September 15, 2024, the population of the United States is 345,810,593. This is based on World meter's analysis of the most recent United Nations data.

The US population is 4.23% of the total world population and ranks third in the world by population. The population density is 98 people per square mile, and 82.4% of the population is urban.

Notorious people who became Saints

The Testimony of Saints Past Life Narrative0
by Father Lee Davis on July 16, 2024

Mary Magdalene's journey from a woman healed of demons to a devoted disciple, supporter of Jesus' ministry, and the first witness to the resurrection offers several timeless lessons:

1. Transformation: Her life reminds us that no one is beyond the reach of God's transformative power. Mary Magdalene's healing and subsequent devotion to Jesus show that personal transformation is possible, regardless of one's past.
2. Faith and Devotion: Her unwavering faith and loyalty, even in the face of adversity, exemplify the depth of true discipleship. Mary Magdalene's presence at the crucifixion and her role as the first to witness and proclaim the resurrection inspire us to remain steadfast in our faith.
3. **Role of Women**: Her story highlights the significant, often overlooked contributions of women in the early church and in faith communities today. Mary Magdalene's support of Jesus' ministry and her pivotal role in the resurrection narrative challenge us to recognize and value the vital contributions of women in all aspects of life.
4. **Witnessing and Proclaiming**: As the "apostle to the apostles," Mary Magdalene's mission to share the news of the resurrection encourages us to be bold in our witness, sharing the message of hope and redemption with others.

Mary Magdalene's life is a powerful narrative of transformation, faith, and devotion. As we continue to explore and understand her story, Mary Magdalene remains a beacon of hope and inspiration, reminding us of the profound impact one person's faith and witness can have on the world.

Mary Magdalene is mentioned in the Bible
Matthew 27:56, 61; 28:1; Mark 15:40, 47, 16:1, 9; Luke 8:2, 24:10;and Jo hn 19:25, 20:1, 11, 18

Saint Paul was a tent maker. It was also thought that he was a member of the Sadducees, who were associates of the High Priest and the chief persecutors of the Christian movement in Jerusalem. (Take note of the fact that images and statues of St. Paul that you see today show him with a sword.) It is possible that he believed that (1) Jewish converts to the new movement did not correctly observe the Jewish law, (2) that they mingled with the Gentile converts too much, (3) or that he did not believe that God chose to favor Jesus by raising Him from the dead.

Paul's persecutions probably found him traveling from synagogue to synagogue urging the punishment of those who believed that Jesus was the Messiah. He urged the punishment of Such Jews by ostracism or by light flogging, or both. He began his persecutions *in* Jerusalem, although he later denied having known any of the followers of Christ in Jerusalem until after his own conversion.

St. Paul's conversion to Christianity is one of the most important events in history. This monumental event occurred during his travel to Damascus. He was on the road to Damascus when suddenly he had a vision that changed his life, his views, and his reason for being. He saw the Lord who came to him in a blinding light. Paul was temporarily blinded by this light, it was so brilliant. He believed that his vision proved that Jesus was the Messiah and the Son of God, and that He would return. He believed that this event was to tell him that he was chosen by God to preach to the Gentiles. At this point he traveled to Arabia, then to Damascus where he remained for three years, after which he went to Jerusalem to meet and get to know the leading apostles there. It was after this that he began his famous missions to the west.

Saint Augustine of Hippo's life before his conversion was marked by a variety of experiences, including:

- A difficult childhood: Despite being raised by a devout Christian mother, Augustine was a difficult child and grew up to be an atheist.

- An immoral life: Augustine led an immoral life from the age of 16, having a child out of wedlock, stealing, and embracing heretical teachings.

- A search for answers: Augustine followed various philosophers but became disillusioned with their teachings. He also spent nine years associated with the Manichean sect, but eventually became aware that they could not provide satisfactory answers to his questions.

- A rhetoric teacher: Augustine taught rhetoric in his native town, Rome, and Milan.

- A relationship with his mother: Augustine's mother, Monica, prayed for his redemption for 17 years.

- An encounter with Saint Ambrose: Augustine met Saint Ambrose, the Bishop of Milan, who was an orator with a commitment to truth.

- An experience with a song: Augustine heard a child singing a song that he thought might be a command from God to open and read the Scriptures.

- A baptism: Augustine was baptized by Bishop Ambrose of Milan at the age of 33.

Thomas Jefferson:

We all know that Jefferson was an imperfect embodiment of America's greatest ideals. He wrote that all men are created equal and owned them, too. Jefferson was America's greatest exemplar of the Enlightenment. He was essentially a pacifist. He took things always by their smooth handle. He believed in civility, order, due process, the rule of law, majority rule, generosity of spirit, and sensitivity to the sensibilities of those around us. He was more likely to write a letter or an essay than throw a brick or wander through the streets of Charlottesville holding burning brands. He knew we must sometimes disagree, but he always hoped we could, as he put it, "disagree as rational friends. "Let us restore to social intercourse that harmony and affection without which liberty and even life itself are but dreary things.

The other moment from Jefferson's life came in 1825. Almost immediately after the University of Virginia opened, there was a student riot. It had the usual features: drunkenness, property damage, general roistering, and a bottle of urine thrown into a professor's private quarters. Some of Jefferson's hand-picked faculty were threatening to quit. When he heard about the incident the ancient Jefferson, now approaching death, saddled up and rode down the mountain to his academical village, gathered the student body in the Rotunda—Jefferson's paean to the Pantheon at Rome—and tried to recall them to good sense. The students refused to listen to the aging patriarch. A witness later wrote, "His lips moved—he essayed to speak—burst into tears & sank back into his seat! The shock was electric!" Jefferson called the student riot "the most painful event of my life." If Jefferson were alive today, he would weep for Charlottesville.

He would weep for the lost promises of our republic.

He would weep for America.

Source*: Charles Wesley Alexander – The American Catholic

George Washington – Valley Forge

"The source for all of this was Charles Wesley Alexander who published this piece in April 1861 at the onset of the Civil War.

There is a document called Washington's Vision that claims to describe a vision that George Washington had at Valley Forge in 1777. The document claims that Washington saw an angel who spoke to him and showed him a vision of the United States, two armies, and the Civil War and World War I.

Here are some other facts about George Washington and religion:

- Catholic support

  Washington was impressed by the support Catholics gave to the American cause during the Revolutionary War. He gave more to

Catholic institutions than to other charities, even though he was supposedly anti-Catholic.

- Anglican

Washington was an Anglican, but he was private about his religious beliefs.

"The last time I ever saw Anthony Sherman was on the Fourth of July, 1859, in Independence Square. He was then ninety-nine years old, his dimming eyes rekindled as he gazed upon Independence Hall, which he had come to visit once more. "I want to tell you an incident of Washington's life one which no one alive knows of except myself; and which, if you live, you will before long see verified."

He said, "From the opening of the Revolution, we experienced all phases of fortune, good and ill. The darkest period we ever had, I think, was when Washington, after several reverses, retreated to Valley Forge, where he resolved to pass the winter of 1777. Ah! I often saw the tears coursing down our dear commander's careworn cheeks, as he conversed with a confidential officer about the condition of his soldiers. You have doubtless heard the story of Washington's going to the thicket to pray. Well, he also used to pray to God in secret for aid and comfort.

"One day, I remember well, the chilly winds whistled through the leafless trees. Though the sky was cloudless and the sun shone brightly, he remained alone in his quarters nearly all afternoon. When he came out, I noticed that his face was a shade paler than usual, and there seemed to be something on his mind of more than ordinary importance. Returning just after dusk, he dispatched an orderly to the quarters of the officer I mentioned who was in attendance at the time. After preliminary conversation of about half an hour, Washington, gazing upon his companion with that strange look of dignity that he alone could command, said to the latter:

"I do not know whether it is due to the anxiety of my mind, or what, but this afternoon, as I was preparing a dispatch, something seemed to disturbed me. Looking up, I beheld, standing opposite me, a singularly beautiful being. So astonished was I, for I had given strict orders not to be disturbed, that it was some moments before I found language to inquire the cause of the visit. A second, a third, and even a fourth time did I repeat my question, but received no answer from my mysterious visitor, except a slight raising of the eyes. By this time I felt strange sensations spreading through me, and I would have risen, but the riveted gaze of the being before me rendered volition impossible. I assayed once more to speak, but my tongue had become useless, as though it had become paralyzed. A new influence, mysterious, potent, irresistible, took possession. All I could do was to gaze steadily, vacantly at my unknown visitor. Gradually the surrounding atmosphere seemed to become filled with sensations, and grew luminous. Everything about me seemed to rarefy, including the mysterious visitor.

"I began to feel as one dying, or rather to experience the sensations which I have sometimes imagined accompany dissolution. I did not think, I did not reason, I did not move; all were alike impossible. I was only conscious of gazing fixedly, vacantly at my companion.

"Presently I heard a voice saying, 'Son of the Republic, look and learn,' while at the same time my visitor extended an arm eastwardly. I now beheld a heavy vapor at some distance rising fold upon fold. This gradually dissipated, and I looked out upon a strange scene. Before me lay spread out in one vast plain all the countries of the world — Europe, Asia, Africa, and America. I saw rolling and tossing between Europe and America the billows of the Atlantic, and between Asia and America lay the Pacific.

"'Son of the Republic,' said the same mysterious voice as before, 'look and learn.' At that moment I beheld a dark, shadowy being as an angel standing, or rather floating, in mid-air between Europe and America. Dipping water out of the ocean in the hollow of his hand, he cast some on Europe. Immediately a cloud raised from these countries, and joined in mid-ocean. For a while it remained stationary, and then moved slowly westward until it enveloped America in its murky folds. Sharp flashes of lightning gleamed through it at intervals, and I heard the smothered groans and cries of the American people. A second time the angel dipped water from the ocean and sprinkled it out as before. The dark cloud was then drawn back to the ocean, in whose billows it sank from view.

"A third time I heard the mysterious voice saying, 'Son of the Republic, look and learn.' I cast my eyes upon America and beheld villages and towns and cities string up one after another until the whole land form the Atlantic to the Pacific was dotted with them. Again I heard the mysterious voice say, 'Son of the Republic, the end of the century cometh; look and learn.' "And this time the dark, shadowy angel turned his face southward, and from Africa I saw an ill-omened specter approach our land. It flitted slowly over every town and city of the latter. The inhabitants presently set themselves in battle against each other. As I continued looking, I saw a bright angel, on whose brow rested a crown of light on which was traced the word 'Union,' bearing the American flag, which he placed between the divided nation. He said, 'Remember, ye are brethren.' Instantly the inhabitants, casting down their weapons, became friends once more, and united around the National Standard.

"Again I heard the mysterious voice saying, 'Son of the Republic, look and learn.' At this the dark, shadowy angel placed a trumpet to his lips and blew three distinct blasts; and taking water from the ocean, he sprinkled it on Europe, Asia, and Africa. Then my eyes beheld a fearful scene. From each of these countries arose thick black clouds that were soon joined into one; and throughout this mass there gleamed a dark red light be which I saw hordes of armed men, who, moving with the cloud, marched by land and sailed by sea to America, which country was enveloped in the volume of cloud. And I dimly saw these vast armies devastate the whole country and burn the villages, towns, and cities that I had beheld springing up."As my ears listened to the thundering of the cannon, the slashing of swords, and the shouts and cries of millions in mortal combat, I again heard the mysterious voice saying, 'Son of the Republic, look and learn.' When the voice had ceased, the dark angel placed his trumpet once more to his mouth and blew a long and fearful blast.

"Instantly a light as of a thousand suns shown down from above me, and pierced and broke into fragments the dark cloud which enveloped America. At the same moment the angel upon whose head still shown the word 'Union' and who bore our national flag in one hand and a sword in the other descended from the heavens attended by legions of white spirits. These immediately joined the inhabitants of America, who I perceived were well-nigh overcome, but who, immediately taking courage again, closed up their broken ranks and renewed the battle. Again, amid the fearful noise of the conflict I heard the mysterious voice saying, 'Son of the Republic, look and learn.' As the voice ceased, the shadowy angel for the last time dipped water from the ocean and sprinkled it upon America. Instantly the dark cloud rolled back, together with the armies it had brought, leaving the inhabitants of the land victorious.

"Then once more, I beheld the villages, towns, and cities springing up where I'd seen them before, while the bright angel, planting the azure standard he had brought in the midst of them, cried with a loud voice: 'While the stars remain, and the heavens send down dew upon the earth, so long shall the Union last.' And taking from his brow the crown on which blazoned the word 'Union,' he placed it upon the standard while the people, kneeling down, said 'Amen.'

"The scene instantly began to fade and dissolve, and I, at last, saw nothing but the rising, curling vapor I had at first beheld. This also disappeared, and I found myself once more gazing upon the mysterious visitor, who in the same voice I had heard before said, 'Son of the Republic, what you have seen is thus interpreted. Three great perils will come upon the Republic. The most fearful is the third, but in this greatest conflict the whole world united shall not prevail against her. Let every child of the Republic learn to live for his God, his land, and the Union.' With these words the vision vanished, and I started from my seat and felt that I had seen a vision wherein had been shown me the birth, progress, and destiny of the United States."

"Such, my friends," said the venerable narrator, "were the words I heard from Washington's own lips, and America will do well to profit by them."The source for all of this was Charles Wesley Alexander who published this piece in April 1861 at the onset of the Civil War. It was written to raise Union morale and was not intended to be taken as an actual vision of Washington. He wrote similar tracts during the War where contemporary Union figures such as Lincoln, McClellan, Grant, etc, received supernatural visions to aid them in the great struggle in which they were engaged. He also wrote tales about female Union soldiers with supernatural powers and a demonic Englishwoman who fought for the Confederacy. That a production from his prolific pen is now regarded as a real vision of Washington by some would no doubt either have vastly amused him or vastly appalled him.

Royal Rulers who became saints

Saint Helena and her son Emperor Constantine (306 -337)
Source: Lives of the Saints by Father Alban Butler
Emperor Constantine ruled for 31 years

Now, Constantius is Emperor as Saint Helena always wished and hoped. Saint Helena had two wishes: that the Edict of the Emperor Diocletian was cancelled setting the Christian free to practice their religion and appointing Constantine officer in his army. The aged and sick Emperor Constantius surprised Saint Helena by making Constantine his successor on his throne. As he was dying, he summoned all his high-ranking commanders and in 306 proclaimed his son Constantine as Emperor of the Roman Empire and Saint Helena fell on her knees, tearfully said to the dying Emperor, "Thank you, Oh thank you, and started to pray. Her conversion to Christianity followed her son becoming emperor. She influenced her son to become Christian and in 313 Emperor Constantine, sole ruler of the Western Roman Empire issued the Edict of Milan which guaranteed religious tolerance for Christians.

In the year 312 Constantine found himself attacked by Emperor Maxentius, ruler of the Eastern Empire, with vastly superior forces, and the very existence of his empire threatened. In this crisis he remembered the Crucified Christian God Whom his mother worshipped, and kneeling down, prayed God to reveal Himself and give him the victory. Suddenly, at noonday, a cross of fire was seen by his army in the calm and cloudless sky, and beneath it the words, *In hoc signo vinces* – "Through this sign thou shall conquer." Constantine made a standard like the cross he had seen, which was borne at the head of his troops; and under this Christian ensign. Maxentius' men saw before them an imposing semi-circle of enemies, white crosses on helmets and shields glistening in the sun, strange banners raised against them. It was not surprising, that on the day after the battle the rumor went around in Rome that an army of 'warriors of light" had come to the help of Constantine and had decided the day for him and his cause. In 323, when Constantine became the sole ruler of the entire Roman Empire, he extended the provisions of the Edict of Milan to the Eastern half of the Empire. After three hundred years of persecution, Christian could finally practice their faith without fear.

 The emperor deeply revered the victory-bearing Sign of the Cross of the Lord, and wanted to find the actual Cross upon which our Lord Jesus Christ was crucified. He sent his mother Helena, to Jerusalem providing her with a letter to Saint Macarius, Patriarch of Jerusalem. After searching the Cross for some time, in 326 Saint Helena was directed to the Temple of Venus. She ordered the temple to be demolished. After praying, the ground began to be excavated. Soon, the Tomb of the Lord was uncovered. Not far from it were three crosses, a board with the inscription ordered by Pilate, and four nails which had pierced the Lord's Body. In order to determine the cross on which t0he Savior had been crucified, St. Macarius alternately touched the crosses to a corpse, When the dead man was touched by the True Cross of the Lord, the body came to life. Another miracle took place, a grievously sick woman, beneath the shadow of the Holy Cross, was healed instantly. Everyone was convinced that the Life-Creating Cross was found.

Some of Constantine's accomplishments include:

- Edict of Milan: In 313, Constantine and the eastern emperor Licinius issued the Edict of Milan, which legalized Christianity and granted freedom of worship throughout the empire.

- Constantinople: Constantine founded the city of Constantinople on the site of Byzantium.

- Arch of Constantine: Constantine ordered the construction of the Arch of Constantine.

- Military restructuring: Constantine restructured the military.

- New money: Constantine created new money to combat inflation.

- Public baths and military stations: Constantine ordered the construction of public baths and military stations.

- Protective wall: Constantine improved the protective wall around Rome.

Constantine I (27 February c. 272 – 22 May 337), also known as Constantine the Great, was a Roman emperor from AD 306 to 337 and the first Roman emperor to convert to Christianity.

- Source: Emperor Constantine - World History
  Encyclopedia – Wikipedia

Saint Henry II – Holy Roman Emperor
Source: Lives of the Saints Father Alban Butler
Saint Henry II ruled for 22 years

⸸St. Henry was born in 6 May 973 in Germany. His father, Duke of Bavaria, because he rebelled against two previous emperors the young Henry was often in exile. This led him to turn to the church finding refuge with St. Wolfgang, Bishop of Ratisbon. St Henry was put under his tuition. Bishop Wolfgang, being prelate, the most eminent in all Germany for learning, piety and zeal, and by his excellent instructions and example made the young prince wonderful progress in learning and in the most perfect practice of Christian virtue.

When his cousin Emperor Otto III died of a fever, leaving no heir, Henry was crowned King of Germany on July 9, 1002 at Mentz. Understanding the precipice of power, he studied the extent and importance of obligations granted to him. His practice of humiliation, prayer and pious meditation, he maintains in his heart the necessary spirit of humility and holy fear. His evenness of temper enable him to bear the tide of prosperity and honor. He endeavored to promote first that all things come from God and belong to God, then the exaltation of his church and the peace and happiness of his people.

In a vision his guardian St Wolfgang, pointing to the words "after six". This sign moved him to   prepared for death, and for six years he continued to watch and prayed and at the end of the sixth year, he found the warning verified in his election as emperor. Trained in the fear of God, he ascended the throne with but one thought "to reign for His Greater Glory". The pagan Slavs were then despoiling the empire. Henry attacked them with a small force; but Angels and Saints were seen leading his troops, and the heathen fled in despair. Holy martyrs Saint Laurence, Saint George and Saint Adrian were seen in battle fighting the pagans.

Henry II ruled over a vast area of Europe consolidating his power, he proceeded to name Bishops who were worthy of that office, he supported monasteries, including the famous Benedictine Abbey. Henry also erected numerous cathedrals, restored churches damaged by heretics, established dioceses and promoted monastic reform. He thought that monasteries were indispensable as centers of prayer and focal points for the civilization of the people. Faith secured in his Empire, Henry was crowned as emperor in 1014 at Saint Peter Basilica by Pope Benedict VIII. It was Henry's custom, on arriving in any town to spend his first night in watching in some church dedicated to our Blessed Mother Mary. As he was praying in Saint Mary Major's, the first night of his arrival in Rome, the great door suddenly by itself opened, he saw "the Eternal Divine Priest Christ Jesus" processed in to say Mass. Saints Laurence and Vincent assisted as deacon and sub-deacon. Saints innumerable filled the church, and Angels sang 0in the choir. After the Gospel, an angel was sent by Our Holy Mother Mary to give Henry the book to kiss. Touching him lightly on the thigh, as the angel did to Jacob, he said "accept this sign of God's love for your chastity and justice;" and from that time the emperor always was lame.

Henry was the first emperor to receive the Golden Globe surmounted by the cross. He wanted to have the seat of the empire in Germany rather than in Rome. He announced his desire to establish a new diocese in Germany: the Diocese of Bamberg, giving the estates to his wife Cunigunde of Luxembourg as her dower upon their marriage. After Easter, Henry II fell ill in Bamberg, he died on July 13, 1024 at the age of 51. Empress Cunigunde arranged for Henry to be interred at Bamberg Cathedral. He left the empire without significant problems, also left the empire without an heir. Both had taken a vow of chastity and because of their piety, they had no royal issues. Their marriage being childless, the Ottonians Dynasty died with Henry. Henry remained celibate all his life also Cunigunde remained a virgin when she died.

⚮ Mother of the King, Queen Blanche of Castile took the Catholic faith seriously, and she instilled deep devotion and piety in her royal son. She is reported to have once told young Louis,"I love you dear son, as much as a mother can love her child; but I would rather see you dead at my feet than that you commit a mortal sin," and he never forgot her words. His mother trained him to be a great leader and a good Christian. At the age of 12 he was crowned King of France and his mother was declared Regent for her son. From his mother, he also learned the most important lesson of all – how to be a saint -

At an early age he often practiced charity, on one occasion, after his crowning celebration, down below his castle he saw ten beggars. He knew no one was so important to the young Louis as those ten beggars. The Lord had healed ten lepers – and one of beggars was a leper. This leper crouched away from the others kept on saying: "Unclean! Unclean!" as a warning to keep people away, which was required at that time. Without a thought for his own well-being, the young king ran down and bent over the leper, lifted his thin hand and kissed it. Louis said: "I have no purse, but when the bread is given out, tell them I asked that you have two portions." The leper, weeping, touched his forehead to the ground, and the crowd shouted "Bravo! Bravo!

On another occasion, after the wedding ceremony with Marguerite, an acolyte stood with a basin of water and a towel for a filthy and old beggar. The beggar was seated on a stool. Louis took the towel and fastened it about his waist. Then kneeling, he lifted one of the old man's feet into the basin. He washed carefully and well. This was something Jesus had done for the apostles, with humility and patience. Raising, he laid his hand on the old man's shoulder, he said,"Thank you, my friend, "Without you to lend me your poor body, I could not perform this blessed work of charity. So you have gained spiritually as I." He, then, took his purse and gave it to the old man and told him when he had spent all this money, to come back for more.

Louis said to his newly betrothed, you will get use to this. Every Friday we will perform this work of charity. You will come to love it as much as I do."

Louis was born on April 25, 1214 at Poissy, near Paris. He was 11 years old when the death of Louis VIII made him king. Because of his minority, ambitious barons tried to rebel again him, but for her mother the Regent Queen Blanche, by several alliances and her courage and diligence overcame the rebels in the field and forced them into submission. Louis was merciful even to the rebels, and by his readiness to receive any proposals of agreement gave proof that he neither sought revenge nor conquest. His mother's influence was to permeate his life, driving him to pursue sanctity and just use of his authority. At the age 19 he married Marguerite of Provence who 14 years old.. The marriage was blessed with a happy union of hearts and 11 children, 5 sons and 6 daughters.

In 1235, having come of age, King Louis received full power as monarch. Louis set about achieving his personal goal of making France one of the foremost Christian kingdoms. One of his very first acts was to build a monastery named Abbey Royaumont, it was one of the many religious foundations he was responsible. He had many sacred relics brought from Israel to France for veneration, his treasures were the Crown of Thorns and a fragment of the True Cross, he housed them in his personal Sainte Chapelle in Paris. This Church was so exquisite that it was copied more than once by his descendants elsewhere.

During the so-called " golden century of Saint Louis", the kingdom of France was at its height un Europe, both politically and economically, Saint Louis was regarded as first among equals, among the kings and rulers on the continent. He commanded the largest army and ruled the largest and wealthiest kingdom, the European center of arts. The foundation for the famous college of theology later known as the Sorbonne were laid in Paris about the year 1257.

Louis was always respectful of the papacy. He and his Queen defended and protected the clergy from barons and royal officers. In 1230 the King forbade all forms of usury, defined at the time as taking of interest. Louis also ordered, at the urging of Pope Gregory IX, because of the Disputation, the burning in Paris in 1243 of manuscript copies of the Talmud. Eventually, the edict against the Talmud was overturned by Gregory IX's successor, Innocent IV. When his courtiers remonstrated with Louis for his law that blasphemers should be branded on the lips, he replied, "I would willingly have my own lips branded to root out blasphemy from my kingdom.

Louis IX took very seriously his mission as "lieutenant of God on Earth, "with which he had been invested when he was crowned in Reims. St. Louis took the Cross for a Crusade when he was 30. His army seized Damietta, Egypt, but not long after, weakened by dysentery, Louis, helping to nurse the sick, fell sick himself and without support, they were surrounded and captured. During his captivity the king recited the Divine Office every day, the Saracen guards listened to his praying. The Saracen guards were amazed that this king never complain and is always patient. Louis obtained the release of the army by giving up the city of Damietta in addition to paying a ransom.

During his first crusade in 1248, Louis was approached by envoys from Eljigidei, the Mongol military commander stationed in Armenia and Persia. Louis sent Andre de Longjumeau, a Dominican priest, as an emissary to the Great Khan Guyuk Khani in Mongolia. Guyuk died before the emissary arrived at his court, instead his Queen Oghul Qaimish, now regent, politely turned down the diplomatic offer.

Following his release from Egyptian captivity, St. Louis spent 4 years in the Latin kingdoms of Acre, Caesarea, and Jaffa, using his wealth to assist the Crusaders in rebuilding their defenses and conducting diplomacy with the Islamic powers of Syria and Egypt. Then, he heard his mother died, who was regent in his absence. In the Spring of 1254 he and his army returned to France. He had been away for 6 years. Disturbed by new Muslim advances in Syria, he led another crusade in 1267, at the age of 41. Louis resolved to land at Tunis, and he ordered his eldest son Philip to join him there. The crusaders, among whom was Prince Edward of England, landed at Carthage July 17, 1270, but disease broke out in the camp. Many died of typhus. It was soon seen that Louis was dying. His final instructions to his children reveal his character as a man. The entire instruction is too long, so here are some of the words he revealed:

"My first instruction is If God send you adversity, receive it in patience and give thanks to our Savior and think you have deserved it, and He will make it turn to your advantage. If God send you prosperity, then thank Him humbly, so that you will not become worse from pride or any other cause, when you ought to be better. For we should not fight against God with His own gifts."

St. Louis received the last sacraments, and called for the Greek ambassadors and urged them to work for reunion with the Church of Rome. As he was dying, he extended his arms in the form of a cross and said: "I will worship at your holy temple, and give glory to thy name."(Ps 5:8). Then he lost his voice for a time, and when he regained it he spoke his last words: "Into thy hands I commend my soul."

St. Louis was devoted to his people, founding hospitals, visiting the sick, and like his patron Saint Francis, caring even for people with leprosy. He is of the patrons of Secular Franciscan Order. Louis united France – lords and townsfolk, peasants and priests and knights - and by the force of his personality and holiness. For many years the nation was at peace. Every day, Louis had 13 special guests from the poor to eat with him, and a large number of poor were served meals near his palace. During Advent and Lent, all who presented themselves were given a meal, and Louis often served them in person. He kept a lists of needy people, whom he regularly relieved, in every province of his dominion.

In an age of great and holy kings, King Louis was undoubtedly one of the greatest. His humility, his love for Christ and His Church, his just rule, and his sacrifices on behalf of his subjects, all leave us an example of sanctity to be imitated. We desperately need great leaders and statesmen like King Louis in our own time – selfless men who are driven by accomplishing the will of God, and not merely by getting power for its own sake.

Amidst the cares of government, St. Louis daily recited the Divine Office and attended 2 Masses and the most glorious churches in France are still monuments of his piety.

Saint Louis died August 25, 1270 and his feast day is August 25. The message we receive from St. Louis is to avoid mortal sin at all cost, and to live in this world with eyes on our true home above.

Priest in tears

"Eucharistic Miracle" Saturday, August 10, 2024 in Bogota, Colombia, during the adoration vigil for peace in Venezuela, The exposed Blessed Sacrament began to palpitate for 20 minutes, more than 300 faithful were present. Priest was in tears.

When you are in line for   Holy Communion
Pray these prayers

Saint Joseph (any patron saint) please accompany me to receive our Lord Jesus worthily
Saint Raphael please accompany me to receive our Lord Jesus worthily
Saint Michael please accompany me to receive our Lord Jesus worthily
Saint Gabriel please accompany me to receive our Lord Jesus worthily
Guardian Angel please accompany me to receive our Lord Jesus worthily

Here are some examples of prayers after receiving the Eucharist:

- Prayer after Holy Communion
  "I am in Jesus and Jesus is in me. Lord Jesus, you are present within me now in my Holy Communion. I adore you, I welcome you, I worship you".

- Thanksgiving After Holy Communion
  "I thank You, Eternal Father, for giving me as the food of my soul, the Body and Blood of Your Only-begotten Son, our Lord Jesus Christ".

- A Prayer of St. Thomas Aquinas After Communion
  "I thank You, Lord, Almighty Father, Everlasting God, for having been pleased, through no merit of mine, but of Your great mercy alone, to feed me".

A Prayer After Hoy Communion

I humbly adore You and offer my praise for this unfathomable mystery that continually nourishes and strengthens me to live in imitation of Christ.

Through participation in the Eucharist, deepen my faith, hope and love. Draw me into greater communion with You and Your Church. Help me live courageously as Your disciple, now sent forth into the world to walk in Your light. I ask this in the name of Your Son Jesus, through the power of the Holy Spirit. Amen.

Source: Cathedral.org – From a Holy Priest

Leading to the Star of Jacob signifying the foretelling of the coming of a Ruler.

It just happened when I was writing and compiling this narrative, this tragic News came up. This was taken from my book Holy Family Exile to Egypt. Saturday, July 13, 2024: Former President Donald J. Trump was shot at a Rally in Butler, Pennsylvania, as an assassination attempt. The bullet crazed at his right cheek and pierced his right ear.

In the Bible, the concept of blood on the right ear (Leviticus 8:22-24 and 14:28) serves as a visible mark of consecration, signifying that the person is dedicated to God's service and has been set apart for a specific purpose. This act represents a physical and spiritual transformation, preparing the individual for their sacred role. Here's a breakdown of the significance: * Right ear: The right ear represents hearing and obedience. In ancient times, the right ear was considered the most important ear, as it was the ear that heard the words of God. * Blood: Blood represents life, sacrifice, and atonement. In this context, blood is a symbol of purification and consecration. * Consecration: Consecration means to set something or someone apart for a specific purpose, making it holy and dedicated to God. In this case, the blood on the right ear signifies that the person is being set apart for a sacred task or role. * Priestly consecration: In Leviticus 8, the blood is applied to the right ear of Aaron and his sons, consecrating them as priests. This act sets them apart as mediators between God and the people. * Purification: In Leviticus 14, the blood is applied to the right ear of the person being cleansed, symbolizing their purification and restoration to the community.

Responsorial Psalm
Luke 1:69-75

*_Blessed be the Lord, the God of Israel! He has visited his people and
redeemed them.*

He has raised up for us a mighty saviour
in the house of David his servant,
as he promised by the lips of holy men,
those who were his prophets from of old.

A saviour who would free us from our foes,
from the hands of all who hate us.
So his love for our fathers is fulfilled
and his holy covenant remembered.

He swore to Abraham our father
to grant us that free from fear,
and saved from the hands of our foes,
we might serve him in holiness and justice
all the days of our life in his presence.

September 28, 2024, the arrival of the star of Jacob was no ordinary star and symbolized the king and divine Messiah was coming. Scientists predict that a Nova in the star system called T Coronae Borealis or TCB will be visible on earth in the month of October TCB will appear 1500 times brighter than usual making it the 50th brightest star in the night sky this Nova may just be the star of Jacob.

[T Coronae Borealis (T CrB) is the name of a binary star and recurrent nova in the constellation Corona Borealis. T CrB is also known as the Blaze Star.]

The most striking feature of the whole section on Balaam is that the God of Israel resorts to a non-Hebrew prophet to convey his will to the Hebrew tribes wandering through the Plains of Moab, specifically regarding their future vis-à-vis other nations. Moreover, God chooses a non-Hebrew prophet to deliver a prophecy pertaining to the time and circumstances of the Messiah's birth. Numbers 24-17: A star shall rise from Jacob, and a scepter shall rise from Israel, that will crush the brows of Moab, and the skull of all the Sethites.

World Press

God's Glory

The Star of Jacob Is Returning After 2000 Years Ago It Will Be Visible to The Naked Eye It Will Be Here by September 28, 2024 Leaves on November.

Therefore, the "star" of Bethlehem, as briefly painted by Matthew, does signify both a phenomenon event and a hint at the "Star of Jacob" prophecy foretelling the emergence of an ideal ruler (cf. Micah 5:2/1 moshel "ruler"), the long-awaited Messiah, emerging out of Jacob, Israel.

@joemac6172 from YouTube

I have been seeing this huge star for the past year now, so it can't be a different star?? I know it is the same star and it's not only in this past month but it had been showing for quite sometime and I knew it had to be a good sign from God praise be to Jesus and our beloved mother who has been sharing the secrets of God's mysteries to the simple and humble of heart.

Jonathan David Cahn

Focused on end times prophecy, Cahn has said that the United States is "on the wrong path" due to the prevalence of abortion, the pursuit of gay rights, and the perceived decline in the public role of religion. He has cast President Donald Trump as a heroic and biblical figure, and has attended Trump's Mar-a-Lago resort with some other activists. Later, he has claimed that President Joe Biden has put the United States under "demonic possession" for lighting up the White House in LGBTQ Pride rainbow color.

This sign the "Star of Jacob" is very significant to Abraham's descendants. "Star of Jacob" prophecy is foretelling the emergence of an ideal ruler (cf. Micah 5:2/1 moshel "ruler"), The long awaited Messiah has come and gone and the Jews still do not believe He is the Messiah. It takes one of Abraham's descendants to show them and inform them. If the Jews knew Jesus was the Messiah, a lot of pain, agony and suffering would not occur.

However, thanks be to God, He has mercy and forgiveness towards the Jewish people who do not believe Jesus is the Son of God. The descendant from Ashkenazi the tribe of Judah could possibly be Donald J Trump.

After 4124 years it seems that God is about to bless one of Abraham's descendants and make him a great nation. God seeing one of Abraham's descendants going through constant persecution, pain, suffering and humiliation, namely Donald J Trump never doubted the gift of God for keeping him alive. God has recognized Donald Trump as a true ruler and would bless Donald Trump as a true ruler of a Great Holy Nation the United States of America according to His will and He would curse all those who oppose him. There was also a spiritual promise that all nations would be blessed through Jesus Christ, who was a descendant of Abraham (Matthew 1:1-16; Luke 3:23-34).

The United States of America ruled by Donald J Trump under God.

Seeking the guidance of Jesus Christ to lead their country's people in a way of God's will. Peace and Prosperity and Loyal Subjects for many years.

I have received God's Greatest Holy Nation inspiration whilst I was in prayer.

September 1, 2024